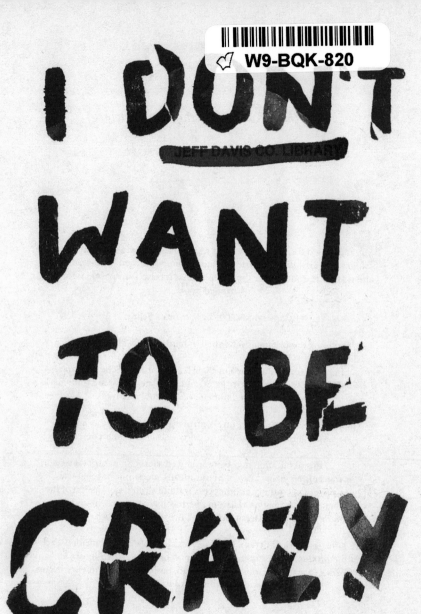

I DON'T WANT TO BE CRAZY

A MEMOIR BY
SAMANTHA SCHUTZ

SCHOLASTIC INC.

For Emily Kozlow — who saw the worst

Copyright © 2006 by Samantha Schutz

This book was originally published in hardcover by PUSH in 2006.

All rights reserved. Published by PUSH, an imprint of Scholastic Inc., *Publishers since 1920.* SCHOLASTIC, PUSH, and associated logos are trademarks and/or registered trademarks of Scholastic Inc.

The publisher does not have any control over and does not assume any responsibility for author or third-party websites or their content.

No part of this publication may be reproduced, stored in a retrieval system, or transmitted in any form or by any means, electronic, mechanical, photocopying, recording, or otherwise, without written permission of the publisher. For information regarding permission, write to Scholastic Inc., Attention: Permissions Department, 557 Broadway, New York, NY 10012.

This book is a work of fiction. Names, characters, places, and incidents are either the product of the author's imagination or are used fictitiously, and any resemblance to actual persons, living or dead, business establishments, events, or locales is entirely coincidental.

ISBN 978-1-338-33749-5

10 9 8 7 6 5 4 3 2 1   19 20 21 22 23

Printed in the U.S.A.   23
This edition first printing 2019

Acknowledgments

I'd like to thank my parents and my sister for being wonderfully strange; all my girls: Adrienne Glasser, Amy Wilson, Annica Lydenberg, Emily Dauber, Emily Haisley, Emily Kozlow, Katie Brian, Melissa Mandelker, and Nicole Duncan for being the best and prettiest girls I know; Barry Goldensohn and Ralph Ciancio for being brilliant and inspiring professors; Dr. Michael Kahan, M.D., and Sharon Flory, L.C.S.W.; and David Levithan, editor and superhero, for understanding how much I needed to tell this story — and how much it needed to be heard.

It takes courage to push yourself to places that you have never been before . . . to test your limits . . . to break through barriers. And the day came when the risk it took to remain tight inside the bud was more painful than the risk it took to blossom.

— Anaïs Nin

Prologue

I can't believe
no one else can hear
I am screaming
inside my head.

Things are moving so fast.
I am going to die.
I am going to die.
I am going to die.
My hands are shaking.
I try to squeeze them, try to make it stop,
but now my fists are shaking,
and this shaking is working its way through me.
It must look like I am having a fit.
I want to let the scream out,
but I think if I start,
I'll never stop.

It's not supposed to be like this.
I am too young to die.
I don't know how to make this end,
and if it doesn't, I'll have to go to a hospital,

be medicated, force-fed soft foods.
I don't want to be that person.
I am not that person.
I am not.
I am not.

Part I

i.

Each day another friend leaves for college.
Yesterday Abe, today Claire,
tomorrow Matt.
When it's my turn,
nobody will be left
to say good-bye to me.

It's crazy that I'm leaving
everything and everyone I know,
but there are things I want to leave behind,
things I don't have room for —
like this version of me,
like Jason.
Sometimes I call him my boyfriend,
but I know better.

I'm excited to leave,
to start something new,
but it scares me.
And what scares me even more
is that things are supposed to get harder than this —
harder than living in my parents' house,
harder than dealing with Jason,

harder than high school.
I can't be a kid anymore.

All my neighborhood friends and I
go to one party after another,
drinking, getting high —
the same stupid stuff we always do
in the playground of P.S. 98
or down at the field.
Now we call them good-bye parties,
but they're really just another excuse to get high.

I am sitting behind the register at the theater
looking out the window
at the cars speeding by,
thinking, I can't believe it's finally over.
I am out of high school.

I'll never again have to wear that polyester kilt
with the stapled hem and melted hole
where Audrey accidentally ashed on me.
I'll never get detention for wearing combat boots
or have to take the Q46 bus halfway across Queens.

6

I don't ever have to sit in the senior lounge
wishing I could play my music
without Justin calling Tori Amos *Tour of My Anus*.
I don't have to pretend to like people
who are assholes and call me flat-chested.
I don't have to be treated like crap
just because I'm not popular.

Applying to college was a disaster.
My parents had their choice for me,
and I had mine.
But since they were paying the bills,
there was no room for compromise.

We fought about my application essay for weeks.
It had to be perfect —
revised and reread dozens of times,
marked up in red pen
until it was bloody.

In the end my personal statement
was more my mother's than my own
and fiction became fact
because it sounded better.

It's been like this
for as long as I can remember —
writing and rewriting homework,
book reports, and papers
until they were not mine —
until they were perfect.

I don't understand
how my teachers never noticed.
How could they believe
all those words were mine?
Every time I handed in a paper
I hoped I'd get caught.

A week before I leave,
Jason picks me up after work
and we go down to the woods
at the edge of the bay
where there's a washed-up diving platform.
The moon is bright enough
that we can find the path,
but I still hold his hand —
let him guide me
around branches and rocks.

When we get to the platform
it's covered with slugs.
We kick them off and lie down.
It doesn't matter
that there are trails of ooze.
It doesn't matter
that it is low tide
and the mosquitoes are out.
All that matters
is that his hands cover me
like my clothes should.

In the morning I wake up, shower,
see that I am covered in bites, some bleeding
from where I must have scratched them in the night.
I spend the day at work
counting bites, rubbing on cortisone,
and thinking of Jason's hands.

It sounds nice,
but it's not.
It sounds easy,
but it isn't.
The next day Jason is a half hour late

to get me from work.
No phone call.
No explanation.
Just like always,
I am an afterthought.
Just like the night he promised
we'd be alone and showed up with two friends
ready to smoke a blunt.
Just like the afternoon
he said he was going to pick me up
after his laundry finished drying
and never showed
because he fell asleep.

It's been like this ever since Christmas,
when he kissed me
and then told me he'd been waiting
a long time to do that.
Ever since then
I've been waiting
for him to do something, anything
to show he cares,
for him to be the one to ask me to hang out,
waiting for the phone to ring,
checking to see if the phone is broken,

or if someone's already on the line.
I'm glad I'm leaving.
I don't want to wait anymore.

I'm surrounded by stacks of towels,
linens still in the package,
jeans and sweaters,
jumbo boxes of tampons,
soap, and shampoo.
I'm listening to Ani DiFranco so loud
my parents are going to start to yell.

By the end of the week
everything needs to be packed
in these giant plastic tubs
like leftovers
and in garbage bags
like trash.

Everything I own,
everything I care about, is at my feet:
a Valentine's Day card from Jason
that reads *I wish for you,*
a collage Claire made for my birthday

of handpainted portraits of the two of us,
a photo of me and Audrey
sitting in the back row of the Q79 bus,
a drawing I made in 1983.

I can't wait
to get out of this room
with its stupid flowered wallpaper,
out of this house
with all its rules,
out of this neighborhood
where everyone knows each other.

I try folding things neatly,
even though I'm a slob.
I am starting something new.
I want to do this right.

A couple of nights before I leave
Jason tries again to get me to have sex with him.
We are in his bed when he gives me a speech
about how I won't want to lose my virginity
to some stranger in college.
He reminds me

that he is here,
next to me,
safe.

But I've already given him everything else.
This is the only thing I have left.

I'm leaving tomorrow
and saying good-bye to Jason tonight.
I don't think I can handle it
if he kisses me.
It will only make things harder.
It will only make me cry
to kiss him,
to feel the emptiness.

I wonder if he feels it.
I wonder if he even cares.

What a fitting ending with Jason.
No hug.
No kiss.
Nothing.

13

Just like always, he was late
and I was pissed.
This time it was the weed's fault.
It knocked him on his ass, hard.
He was pale, almost green.
He could barely speak.
His best friend Nate was there
to confirm the story.
I could see in Jason's face
that it was the truth,
but it was too late.

I can't fall asleep.
It's like the night before camp,
except I don't come home after six weeks.
It's like the night before an exam
that I haven't studied for enough.
It's like the night before my birthday,
knowing my expectations will never be lived up to.
It's like the night before a vacation,
and I'm terrified to fly.

It is the night before everything.

14

ii.

My roommate Sarah is in our dorm room
when my parents and I get upstairs with the first load.
She is one of the kids I met
at the overnight open house in the spring.
None of us knew if we'd been accepted
and it was strange to think
that we might make friends we'd never see again.
That night, in the woods, behind one of the dorms,
a bunch of us got stoned and swore that if we got in,
we'd go, be friends, request to be roommates —
Sarah and I,
Josh and Adam.
We'd be safe from the freaks.

When I walk into our dorm room,
I drop my stuff on the floor,
and Sarah and I scream and hug.
I can't believe we are really here,
that all of this is finally starting.

Sarah's stuff is already unpacked
and neatly laid out.

She's managed to make her side of the room into a home.
I can't believe she moved in by herself.

She is quick to excuse herself.
Maybe she can tell that my family is the type
to scream and yell no matter what we do.
Maybe she wants to leave before we ask her to help.
Either way, I'm jealous.

We carry everything up the five flights
because the elevators are backed up.
All my clothes are packed in garbage bags.
My life looks like a dump.

My mother carries a lamp,
then positions herself on the extra-long twin bed.
She supervises for the rest of the afternoon
as my father and I go back and forth
to the Volvo and up and down the stairs.

I wish I didn't have to do this with my parents.
I wish we didn't have to fight
about where everything goes
and have the other kids in my suite hear
and think I am a baby.

My parents leave after the big stuff is in place,
the photos and posters are hung and level,
and my father has changed into a clean polo shirt.

I am finally alone
and it is wonderfully quiet.

That first night Sarah goes out
and Josh comes over.
We've e-mailed since the spring,
exchanged stupid high school stories,
recommended books and CDs,
and speculated on what it would be like
when we actually got to school.

We smoke a joint
and Josh lies down in Sarah's bed —
eyes shut, hands folded across his chest
with his cigarette between his fingers.
He doesn't move for a long time.

"Josh?" No answer.
Louder, "Josh?"
No answer.

17

Is he sleeping? Dead?
I go over to see if he is breathing,
but I am too high to tell.

I lean in closer,
and closer.
I am going to have to put a mirror under his nose.
I can't believe that I killed someone
my first night of college.

I am just inches from Josh's face
when he opens one eye
and smiles at me.
I say, "I thought you were dead."
He starts laughing
and I fall back on my ass
and laugh harder
than I have ever laughed before.

When I met Adam in the spring
there was an instant attraction.
I felt it the first minute I saw him —
the back of him, really.

18

I was walking behind him during the campus tour,
watching his hair swish.
That night we stayed up until four in the morning,
and talked about high school
and wanting to get out of our parents' houses.
I knew he felt the connection too,
but he had a girlfriend
and I had Jason,
so we just slept on nearby couches.

The night after I move into the dorm,
Adam and I go for a walk
while everyone else is at the freshman meet-and-greet.
It's the first time we've spoken since the spring.
He doesn't have a girlfriend anymore
and we kiss in the grass
by one of the outdoor sculptures —
giant yellow metal beams
that look like reaching legs.
We can hear laughing and cheering
coming from the party across the green.
I feel like the cheering is for me,
for us.

This campus is tiny compared to others I've seen,
but it's still a mystery to navigate.
They've given us a map
that I wouldn't be caught dead with
so there's no chance of getting through the day
without asking where something is.

The dining hall is the worst.
It's packed with people —
people who know their way around,
who have friends,
who know where they like to sit
and how to balance their tray
without spilling their coffee
into their cereal.

In high school I knew the rules.
I knew which girls were my friends
and which ones were fake.
I knew the fastest way
to spread a rumor was to tell Lauren
and the fastest way to the lunchroom
was to take the hallway by art class.
I knew my friends sat at the last table on the left
and the cool kids sat at the last table on the right.

I knew that after lunch
my friends hung out in the stairway by the gym,
and if you were careful
you could slip out the East exit
to smoke a cigarette.

Part of my financial aid package
is a job in Food Services.
I was a waitress a few summers ago,
but this is humiliating.
I wear an apron, rubber gloves,
carry food back and forth,
clean up tables,
scrape uneaten food off plates.
I go home stinking
like food and sweat and steam.
I'm actually glad we have to wear a baseball cap.
At least I can pull it down over my eyes.

Jason's photo is tacked
to the bulletin board above my desk.
It's in a corner almost completely covered
by bits of paper with phone numbers,

postcards from friends, and other junk.
I'm sure nobody would even notice him
in all that mess, but he's there.

I miss him.
I hear myself say that
and I know it's ridiculous.
How could I miss someone who was never there?
Especially since I just hooked up with Adam,
but I do.
I miss things about Jason that used to drive me crazy,
like how he never gets angry.
I wish I could be calm all the time,
never neurotic, never obsessive.
I miss how things were familiar with him,
even if it was the familiar feeling
of being let down.

Living with Sarah the first few weeks
is like an extended sleepover party.
We put on mud masks,
sit around, smoke cigarettes, get high,
and listen to the Violent Femmes.

Our dorm room isn't big,
but at least we're not in a triple or a quad.
Sarah and I have been moving around our furniture
to get the room just right.
Now our beds are on opposite sides of the room
and there is some sense of privacy.

The best part of our room is the window seat.
Every room on campus has one,
but ours looks out into the woods.
The leaves have already started to change color.

I can be anything I want here.
No one has to know
that I wasn't popular in high school,
that I've never stayed out all night,
that I'm a virgin,
that everything I see reminds me of Jason.

I am born again here.
I'm taking art classes, writing classes, dance classes —
all the things there was no room for before.
I reread Anaïs Nin's journals
and write in my own

23

sitting underneath this one tree on the green
with a curved trunk that perfectly fits my back.

I am curled up in my window seat
watching some kids playing Frisbee
when my parents call.
They say my sister isn't going back
for her junior year of college.
They say she needs to take some time off
and will be moving home to figure things out.
I imagine her back in our house, with our parents,
and it makes me feel like I am the older sister.

Then they ask how classes are,
how bad working in the dining hall really is.
They want to know if I've made any nice friends,
or met any nice boys,
and before we get off the phone
they say, "It's all up to you.
You're the one in school now."

I think it's supposed to be a joke,
but it's really not funny.

Meeting new people
feels like dating.
I try to find someone I like,
casually start a conversation,
and hope we have things in common.
Only sometimes when I talk to people
I have no idea what they're saying.
I only hear my voice in my head
as their lips move, telling me
if they looked hard enough
they would see fear behind my eyes.

Things move fast here.
Adam's already ended things,
saying, "This is too much, too soon."
It was just like when Jason and I broke up
for the first time, a few weeks before my prom.
As he told me that he couldn't deal with me
trying to deal with him,
I tuned him out, focused on some leaves
blowing back and forth.
I did it again in Adam's room,
stared at his leopard-print sheets

and thought to myself,
my heart can't take this again.

The weather has turned
and Sarah and I put on jackets
before we leave for an off-campus party.
It's dark —
not like New York City dark,
but pitch-black-middle-of-nowhere dark.
It feels like when Claire and I snuck out at camp,
only this time we aren't going to get caught
and I can smell dry leaves in the air
instead of earthy humidity.

We cut through the trees and someone's backyard
and end up on a gravel road.
I can see the house in the distance,
smell the smoke from the bonfire,
and hear the hum of people and music.

It feels weird being here,
watching people talk —
people who must know each other.
I try to look comfortable.

26

I try to look relaxed.
I try to drink the beer,
but I can't stand still.

Sarah and I walk around
and meet a pair of freshmen, Brian and Steve.
I start talking to Brian,
manage to get down my beer, fill my cup again,
and lose Sarah.

Brian walks me back to my room
and before I know it, we are kissing
and my top is off.
It feels good to kiss him,
to have his weight on top of me.

We are only kissing a few minutes
before he goes to unbutton my jeans.
I pull his hand back
and he lets it get tangled in my hair.
It doesn't take long
before he is back at my pants.
I move his hand, but he tries again.
I break away and just stare at him.

Is he stupid?
When I tell him to go
he gives me this wet-eyed-puppy look,
gets out of bed, picks up his sweatshirt,
and leaves.

I move through friends quickly.
I rarely see Josh anymore
and things with Sarah aren't as easy
as I thought they would be.
We barely talk now.

We are all looking for someone
to stay with,
someone to be permanent.
The possibilities are overwhelming,
they make me restless.
There were forty kids in my graduating class
and here there are more than seven hundred.

I hang out inseparably with someone
for a few days.
We devour each other,

tell all our stories,
and then move on.

Things here are not stable.

I think I might be turning into a slut.
I stay out late,
don't tell anyone where I'm going
or where I've been.

It's barely been two months
and I've hooked up with four guys:
Adam;
Brian;
Tim, who kissed like a frog;
Bob, who didn't believe I was a virgin.

I'm not used to there being so many guys around,
so many parties, so many people who don't know me.

The not-so-funny part about Adam
is that now he's got a girlfriend
only a few weeks after telling me

he didn't want a relationship.
She's gorgeous, with blond hair,
green eyes, big tits.

At first I thought
he was a lying shit.
But now I see
he just didn't want
a relationship with me.

This strange thing happens
when I am lying in bed with a guy.
I cannot breathe.
My breaths are either too deep
or too shallow.
Too slow or too quick.

Feeling the guy's chest rise against
my back confuses my own rhythms.
I feel like I have to match his
and I can never seem to catch up.
I just lie there, waiting
for our breaths to sync
or to be able to pull myself away

enough to breathe on my own,
uninfluenced.

It's crazy, but I miss Jason.
With him there were never any surprises.
I could always count on him letting me down.

I shut my eyes
and I see Jason.
I see his skin.
I can feel him kissing me.

I should take down his picture.
It shouldn't even be here.

I don't understand what's happening.
I am sitting in Writing Seminar
and it feels like my hands are shaking,
like I've got a tremor.
I try hard to focus, stare at my hands,
but I can't tell whether or not they're shaking.
I don't understand why I can't tell.
I should be able to tell

if my own hands are shaking.
My eyesight can't be trusted.
I'd try sitting on my hands,
but that would make people stare,
if they haven't already noticed the shaking.
I try clasping my hands together,
but that's no good, either.
I can see myself with my hands together,
banging them up and down on the desk
like a piston, like a cartoon sledgehammer.
I see myself doing it,
but I know I'm not.
I can't be.
If I were, people would be staring.

When class is over,
I am tired and sweaty.
I didn't see anyone looking at me,
so I must not have done anything crazy.
Maybe I'm getting sick
or maybe I'm finally addicted to cigarettes.
This feeling, the sweating, the shaking —
it must be a nicotine fit.

I go outside with the other smokers,
suck down a few cigarettes before class,
hoping it will make me feel better,
hoping it will calm my nerves.

A friend of Sarah's from psych class
comes by to pick her up for a party.
Her name is Rebecca.
When I introduce myself
she says that we've met before —
that she remembers my eyes.
I feel kind of stupid
for not remembering her,
but she doesn't seem to care
and invites me to go with them to the party.

When we get there,
Rebecca and Sarah start dancing.
I lean on one of the speakers instead,
let the bass crawl over my back like fingers
and watch kids in big pants
dance in the light and smoke.

Rebecca grabs my hand
and pulls me onto the dance floor.
I can't stop watching the people around me —
watching what they do,
watching to see if they are watching me
dancing like an idiot.

Rebecca is dancing with her eyes shut
and she is smiling.
She doesn't care what anyone thinks
and it is amazing.

Rebecca and her friends
have been together since the first week.
There's her roommate Rachel,
and Amanda, Tara, and Jennifer.
We all hang out in Rebecca's room and they joke about
how they stopped hanging out with this crazy girl Monica
at the same time they started hanging out with me —
like I took her spot.

Being with them is like walking in
after a play has already started.
You try to slip in quietly and find your seat,

but people turn around,
give you dirty looks,
and whisper to their neighbors
about how rude you are.

A few months ago,
leaving for college seemed glamorous,
but now it's hard to believe
that this little dorm room,
with its scratchy sheets
and a lock that sticks,
is home.

It's hard to accept
that this is my new life,
that these are my new friends.

I am one in many here.
There are dozens here as good as me,
even more who are smarter,
funnier, prettier.
And it scares me
because before I stuck out
and now I blend in

like a pair of khakis
and a baseball cap
at a keg party.

I can't sit still in class.
I can't hear what the teacher is saying.
All I can hear is my voice in my head
telling me that things are not right —
that I am not right.
I am trapped in this classroom.
It feels like something
is trying to push its way out of me,
out of my chest.
I feel like everyone can see it bubbling up,
like they're waiting for me to burst,
to boil over.

I have to get out of here.
I fake a coughing fit and leave,
but once I get in the hallway
I realize I'm still trapped —
stuck inside of this shaking, sweating body.
I'd rip my skin off if I could.
The only place that seems safe

is the bathroom.
Sitting in a stall, with my chest on my thighs,
I try to breathe,
But the more I think about my breathing,
the more I feel like I can't breathe.
It feels like I have a raging fever,
like my insides are melting.
This must be what it feels like
the moment before you die.

I have been telling myself
that these feelings are new,
but they aren't.
I just didn't connect them before.

I felt it the first time I smoked pot junior year.
At first things were fun,
but then everything broke.

It felt like my chest caved in
and I couldn't tell the difference
between the bass in the music
and a car alarm going off outside.
I couldn't get my mind to stop racing.

I felt like I had no control over my body —
like my arms and legs were twitching.
I thought I was going to have to go to the hospital.
I thought I was going to die.
I told myself it was the pot.

But it happened again,
before college,
when I wasn't high.
I was in Staples with my dad,
shopping for school supplies.

All of a sudden the ground felt soft
and the sounds around me
were too fast and too slow
at the same time.

I thought I would lose control,
do something crazy — start screaming
right there in the pen aisle.
My dad would know.
Everyone would know.

Now this feeling follows me
everywhere I go.

It clings to me,
makes my skin crawl,
makes my skin burn
when I walk across campus,
when I check books out of the library,
when I talk to my friends.
It sits with me in class,
whispers in my ear,
tells me that I shouldn't be here.

iii.

Please God make this feeling stop.
I can't take it.
Breathe.
Breathe.
Breathe.
Make it stop.
Please.
Must concentrate on something,
anything.

8:00 A.M.
Smack alarm clock.
Haul ass out of bed.
Shower with very hot water.

8:23 A.M.
Dress.
Paint over dark circles under eyes.
Add color to cheeks.

8:47 A.M.
Eat breakfast alone.

40

Avoid caffeine.
Try to ignore all the noise.

9:03 A.M.
Smoke cigarette.
Go to Writing Seminar.

9:34 A.M.
Feel light-headed.
Feel like passing out.
Fake coughing fit.
Leave class.
Drink water.
Go to bathroom.
Pull down pants.
Sit on toilet.
Put chest on thighs.
Stare at tiles.
Breathe deeply.
Breathe deeply.

9:39 A.M.
Get a grip.
Return to class.

10:00 A.M.
Go back to dorm room.
Get under covers.
Sleep.

12:45 P.M.
Eat lunch with friends.
Try to ignore the noise.

1:20 P.M.
Smoke cigarette.
Go to Freshman Seminar.

1:46 P.M.
Feel like people are staring.
Feel hot.
Feel cold.
Feel out of control.
Fake coughing fit.
Leave class.
Drink water.
Go to bathroom.
Pull down pants.
Sit on toilet.

Put chest on thighs.
Stare at tiles.
Breathe deeply.
Breathe deeply.

1:54 P.M.
Get a grip.
Return to class.

There's this warm white light
that comes in the window
of the waiting room in Health Services.
I've been in a bunch of times
for back pain, sinus pressure, dizziness,
a hemorrhoid that I thought was ass cancer.

I like how the blood pressure cuff feels
tight around my arm,
the way the nurses put the cold stethoscope
to my chest and listen,
listen,
listen.

43

Rebecca, her friends, and I
hang out a lot now,
but I'm pretty sure they think I'm crazy.
One minute I'm fine, talking about homework,
eating lasagna in the dining hall,
and the next I'm complaining
about how dim the lighting is
and running out the door
to get back to my room
and under the covers.

We go to Freshman Seminar together,
but sitting with half the freshman class
crammed into the theater is more than I can take.
Sometimes I go to the bathroom
and don't come back.

I have moved from the front row
of all my classes to the back.
I can't take the feeling of people
looking at me, burning holes in my back.
Back here I can hide
my shaking hands and feet.

I have resigned myself
to the fact that I have gone insane.
I am too tired
to keep fighting
the empty feeling in my stomach
and the buzzing in my head.

This was not supposed to be how things turned out.
There were steps taken, expectations —
a specialized kindergarten and elementary school,
a prestigious private high school
complete with a kilt and knee socks,
summer study programs disguised as camp.

This is not
how things are supposed to be.

Sitting in class has become dangerous.
If I'm not worried about my arms or legs twitching,
I'm worried about screaming out
embarrassing things about myself.

I feel like a marionette —
like someone else is pulling the strings
and I have no choice but to comply.

I've started telling my teachers,
the ones who look like they care
and the ones I care about,
that I am claustrophobic,
because some problems
are easier to talk about than others.

I tell them, "Sometimes I need to leave, get some air."
And when I say, "Don't worry, it isn't your lecture,"
we share a laugh
and I am thankful for my half-truth
because it feels good to confess something.

Not long after I tell one of my English teachers,
there is a note on our door.
Class has been moved across campus to a bigger room.
He never says it was because of me,
but I like to think it was.

Still, it doesn't take long
before I have to leave class,
get some water, sit on the toilet,
and stare at the tiles on the floor
until it is safe to return.

I am in Health Services again,
waiting for the nurse to look me over
with her heavily shadowed eyes,
to take my temperature,
measure my pressure,
listen to my heart and lungs,
to tell me with her sticky pink lips
that I am okay,
when I see a poster on the wall
that says, *Having Panic Attacks?*

For the first time in weeks
things make sense.

It is surprisingly easy.
I walk across the hall to the Counseling Center
and make an appointment.
Two days later I'm at the therapist's office

47

and I'm not sure when to begin.
I sit down in a deep, comfortable chair
facing a picture window with a view
of the snow that has come too early.
Jean is sitting in an identical chair across from me.

She asks, "What brings you here today, Samantha?"
and there is something about the way she says my name
that sounds empty.
It is a simple question,
but I don't have a simple answer.
I tell her I've been freaking out,
but she wants to know what that means.
I say, sometimes I feel out of control,
like I am going crazy when I'm in class,
or the dining hall, and sometimes when I get stoned.
And I start crying, just like that.
All I can think is,
she doesn't know me.

I am sweating a lot, and I wonder if she can tell.
We go on like that for a while.
She asks me questions
about my friends and family

and where I'm from
and I answer, sweat, and blow my nose.

I don't tell her everything.
A lot of it is embarrassing
and she is a stranger,
but I tell her enough to feel lighter.

The psychiatrist's office
is smaller, darker.
There is a regular chair
next to his desk for me.
He has already talked to my therapist
but wants to hear from me
what I have been feeling
and how long I have been feeling it.
After fifteen minutes
I leave with a prescription.

***The Diagnostic and Statistical Manual of Mental Disorders* says**
anxiety disorders include:
panic disorder with and without agoraphobia,

49

agoraphobia with and without panic disorder,
generalized anxiety disorder,
specific phobia,
obsessive-compulsive disorder,
post-traumatic stress disorder.
I am
panic disorder
without agoraphobia.

I qualify because I have experienced
more than two
unexpected panic attacks
in six months
and have persistent concern
about having other attacks.

Sometimes I have five a day.

Panic attacks are
intense periods of fear or discomfort
with at least four symptoms including:
palpitations,
sweating,
trembling,

50

shortness of breath,
sensations of choking or smothering,
chest pain,
nausea,
gastrointestinal distress,
dizziness,
light-headedness,
tingling sensations,
chills,
blushing
hot flashes.
I have all of them
except for chest pains.

I report feelings of
dying,
going crazy,
losing control of emotions and behavior.
I have the urge to
escape or flee
the place where the attack began.

This is my life.

The next time I see Jean she explains
that panic attacks
are part of "fight or flight,"
the body's natural reaction to danger,
only I get confused.
I think there's danger when there isn't.
I want to run.
I want to scream.

She says it's like a switch —
a big red PANIC switch —
gets flipped in my head
and I can't turn it off.

She says we're going to figure out
how to turn it off.

Things I hate:
Dimly lit rooms
Music that is so loud I can't hear anything else
Letting doors close in front of me
Walking across the dining hall
Sitting in front rows
Having diarrhea all the time

Crowded rooms
Falling asleep in front of anyone
The weight I've gained since September
People staring at me
Feeling like I am going to faint
The sound of a CD skipping
Facing a wall at a restaurant
Sleeping with the pattern on my comforter upside down

Klonopin 0.5 mg.
I take one in the morning
and one at night.
It makes me sleep,
makes me get drunk from one drink,
makes the panic a voice in the distance —
loud enough to hear,
but quiet enough to ignore.

I talk to Jean a lot about my family.
There are four of us:
Me, my dad, my mom, and sister.
That's it.
We are alone —

flanked by dysfunction on all sides.
All four grandparents are dead.
My father's sisters are strangers to us
and maybe to him too.
My mother's sister
forbids all contact
and her children are too old to care.
I could walk past all six of my cousins on the street
and never know it.

I hear stories from my mom
about why things are the way they are
and take them with a grain of salt,
knowing we can't be completely without blame.
I wonder
what's so wrong with us
that we have no family?

I am on my way home for Thanksgiving.
I'll be there in a few minutes
and I am scared
that there will be a DO NOT ENTER sign on the door.
I am scared that this is not my home anymore,
that it is just a place with a spare bed.

The moment I drove away in September
I felt like someone was following our car
with an eraser, rubbing out my old life.
Only what was ahead meant anything.

All I want to do is see Jason.
Being here in my room,
where we were together so many times, is hard.
My foundation is in this house, in this neighborhood,
but I feel it crumbling —
it cannot hold this weight.
I hate this.
I hate that I want to hold Jason again.
I hate that I am desperate
and predictable.

I feel guilty sitting across the dining room table
and not telling my parents
that I have a therapist,
that I am on medication,
and that things are such a mess.
But I don't want them to worry.
I don't want them to think
that I can't handle things.

Because I can.
I am.
Things may be bad
but I am trying to make them better.

We go around the Thanksgiving table
saying what we are thankful for.
I don't want it to be my turn.
I don't want to say something generic
like, I am thankful to have my family together,
when we're not all here.
What I want to say is,
I am thankful for Rebecca's support,
for Klonopin,
for Jean.

Being back home is wonderful
and awful.
I'm glad to see my friends,
glad to not have to do work,
but being back in this house,
being treated like a child
and given a curfew

after I've been on my own
is unbearable.

Audrey is having some kids over.
Her parents don't seem to care what we do.
We make a weak attempt to blow smoke out the cellar door,
but the basement still stinks like cigarettes
and the sound of beers clinking is unmistakable.

Jason doesn't show and this feeling
of being alone is familiar.
When a joint gets passed around
there's no reason to say no.
I spend most of the night on the couch
talking to Nate, Jason's best friend.
I don't think I ever realized
how Nate's eyes are crisp blue
and that he speaks softly, like he's whispering,
like he's afraid someone will hear.

Matt comes over and sits on the other side of me,
interrupts, starts flirting,
tells me how good it is to see me, how good I look.

Nate can't compete and I can't resist.
When Matt makes his move
all three of us know what's happening.
I can see the hurt in Nate's eyes,
but I need to be with someone.

The next night I am in Jason's car.
I am staring at the bay
through his windshield,
protected from the wind and cold.
I wonder if he knows I was with Matt
and I can't decide which would be worse:
him knowing or not.

I think my love for Jason
was really envy.
He's careless, reckless, irresponsible,
and at the same time irresistible.

Two days later I'm back at Audrey's.
There are just a few of us.
I am on the couch, sandwiched tightly between Abe,
the first boy I ever kissed, and Nate.

We are talking about kissing.
I say Abe bites when he kisses
and Nate smiles, says he is gentle.
They have a drunken debate over who is a better kisser
and decide the only way to settle it
is to elect me judge.

Abe and I kiss first
and I am smiling so wide
it is difficult to kiss.
Abe still bites, but this time he is more careful —
only lightly tugs on my lower lip.
I can feel Nate watching us.
I think, this is ridiculous,
but I like that they are fighting for my attention.
Abe smiles, like it's a job well done,
and I turn to Nate and lean in.
All I can think is, I've never been this near to him
and he smells like clean laundry and deodorant.
His mouth is soft, his kiss
is barely there,
and my chest aches.
It is no contest.

My parents and I are in the car
on the way to a post-Thanksgiving party.
They talk about what they are going to say
if someone asks why my sister is not in school.
I don't understand why saying she's taking time off
isn't good enough.
I swear to them
if they make anything up,
I will tell the truth
and everyone at the party will know
that they are liars
and that we aren't perfect.

They don't say a word at the party
and maybe to prove how imperfect I am
I tell them in the car on the way home
that I have panic disorder,
that I had a panic attack at the party,
that I have a therapist
and a psychiatrist,
that I am on medication.

They want information.
They want to understand.

My mother cries, says she should have seen it.
When I tell them about the stress
and the pressure they put on me, they say
not to take everything they say so seriously.

The next morning
Amanda comes to drive me back to school.
My mother has not spoken to me since last night.
When I hear Amanda pull into the driveway
I hug my father good-bye.
He instructs me to say good-bye to my mother
as if I wouldn't.
When I kiss her on the cheek and turn to leave
she is silent.
My stomach turns inside out.
I am going to puke,
but not here,
not in this house.

I am on my way home,
but I don't know where home is.
Is it my parents' house?
Is it school?
I am too tired.

61

It hurts to think.
It hurts to care.
My eyes won't stay open.
My hands keep shaking.
I can't think —
too much noise,
too much clutter.

At my next appointment with Jean
I tell her what happened with my parents.
I wear my mother's silence like a badge —
like an *I told you so.*
My mother must think I'm blaming them,
but that's not what I tried to say.
I wanted them to understand
that their words have weight —
that the things they do and say
contribute to my anxiety.
Only she didn't hear it that way.
She must have been thinking,
How could you have problems?
Your grandmother grew up poor
and she never complained.
We have given you everything
you ever needed, ever wanted.

We have created a stable home life for you.
Your father and I are not divorced.
We are not alcoholics or drug addicts.
Your father doesn't beat me.
What could possibly be so wrong with your life?

iv.

The deeper we get into winter
the quieter things become.
I don't have as much anxiety
as I did in September.
In its place is exhaustion
and a different kind of fear.

I am scared
that the only reason I am getting better
is because of these little yellow pills,
that nothing has really changed
except biology,
that the pills are a mask,
that I am fooling myself
into feeling better,
that each day I get more addicted,
that I will be medicated
for the rest of my life.

I see the same faces every day
as I walk the snow-covered paths to class.
People I know nod and say, "What's up?"

64

only it's not really a question
and they don't want a real answer.
No one wants to know how tired I am,
that I just got through having another panic attack,
that I'm perpetually late,
that I can't look at food,
that I feel ugly.

Walking down the narrow path,
there is not enough space for this.
So I smile the smile I have perfected
and reply "hey" like everyone else.
I return my focus back down to the pavement
and watch for ice, the black kind
that you never see until it's too late.

Most days it feels like I am watching a movie
where the sound isn't in sync,
the speed is all wrong.
Either I'm moving too quickly
and the world is dripping along,
or the world is moving too quickly, cosmic,
and I'm oozing like a slug
barely able to pull my own weight.

It's best if I keep moving
because if I stopped and stood still
people would see me shaking.

Nate and I talk on the phone now
about everything but Jason.
We stay on the phone for hours at a time.
He trusts me, tells me everything —
even the worst bits about himself
and his family,
and his ex-girlfriend he can't move past.
It makes me like him even more.

It is after noon
and I haven't spoken yet.
I have early classes on Wednesdays
and was out before the rest of my suite was awake.
I didn't see anyone at breakfast
and my first classes were lectures.
I feel wrapped tightly, sealed.

Today is hurried.
There is no time for lunch,

only a piece of someone's birthday cake.
When the sugar hits, I feel hot and sick —
like I am going to pass out.

I am with Rebecca, Rachel, and Jennifer
in the dining hall for dinner.
We are supposed to go to a party later.
They are talking about what they are going to wear
and who is going to be there
as I try to force down real food
and give my body what it wants,
but the lights are too dim
and the hum of people talking is like a swarm of bees.

I know I feel this sick because I haven't eaten much.
I know that.
It makes sense, it is logical,
but there is this other part of me,
this really loud part, that is screaming,
"Something is wrong.
You are seriously sick,
the kind of sick that comes out of nowhere and kills you
before you even have the chance to get to a doctor."
But then I think of the cake,
and my empty stomach, and logic,

and I tell myself that I am okay.
But I must not look okay
because Rebecca has realized that something is wrong
and when she leans in to talk to me,
the other girls see it too.
Now I am the center of attention.
My craziness is the center of attention.
They all agree that it is the cake, that I really am okay,
but the voice in my head is louder than theirs
and I leave for Health Services
and Rebecca comes with me.

Coming home for winter break is like regression.
I feel like that high school girl forced to wear plaid,
forced in the door by midnight.
I feel like I cannot speak.
My voice is muffled
and the more I am stifled,
the more I cry like a child.

Little yellow pills
for the one who cannot control her adrenaline, her fear.
Little yellow pills
for a child who cannot deal with being an adult.

Little yellow pills
to make me forget.

I take the pills to protect myself,
but are they necessary?
Protection does not come in a bottle.
It is in me,
in my actions,
in my thoughts.
I am the best medicine for myself.

I am the cure
and the disease.

A few days after I get home
my mother wants to talk,
wants to know what a panic attack feels like,
wants to know if it hurts.

When I was sixteen my parents found my stash
and my mother admitted to smoking pot three times.
Now I ask her if she ever had a bad high, freaked out,
because it feels a lot like that.
She says no.

I ask her to think of a time when she was really scared.
She says once she thought she was being followed.
I tell her to remember how it felt —
the terror, the sweat, the heart racing —
to feel it now, in the living room
with the Persian rugs and antiques.

She doesn't understand.
Why would she feel it now,
in her own house, where she is safe?

I tell her
that's a panic attack.

Nate's basement has wood paneling
and smells like mildew.
The couches are covered with faded floral blankets
and this time when we kiss
no one is watching.

For every part of me
there is a part of him to match.
His body fits with mine
so quietly, so comfortably.

70

Later, I am searching
for my underwear,
my socks, my belt,
clawing the carpet for the sticks that held my hair up,
searching for the bits to put myself back together.
My rings are on the table, my shoes
are on the opposite side of the room.
This fit scares me
into silence.

Isn't the point of going away to college
to learn, to become an adult, to be independent?
But when I come home and my parents rein me in
and make sure they know where I am at all times
they take all that away from me.
Don't they trust me?
Do they still think I need to hold their hands?
They'll never let me go.
They'll always be there
to catch me,
to grab me,
to pull me from all sides,
to push me in the direction of their choice.
What about my choice?

71

What about the fact that I can make it on my own?
Can't they see that I'm okay
and the only disasters happened
when I was living with them?

Claire and I watch our camp video
and when I look at my face
and my eyes, I feel bad
because I know what's in store for me in a few years.
I study my movements.
I look for a precursor to my anxiety.
I am not as outgoing as Claire, but no one is.
When the camera is on me
I constantly flip my long brown hair
and never stay in frame very long.
But I look normal.
I look fourteen and as awkward as everyone else.

I think about other things
that could explain what's happened to me.
When I was little I used to walk into mirrors.
I was also scared of the dark
and bridges and elevators.

When I was about thirteen
I was so nervous before flying
that I wrote a will on pale blue stationery
the night before a family vacation.
I addressed separate notes to all my friends and family
and doled out my journals, my jewelry,
and the money in my miniature safe.
I remember crying as I wrote.
I couldn't stop imagining
    our plane crashing into the ocean.
I hid the notes in a book on my shelf.
I still can't remember which book they're in
and I wonder what my parents will think
if they ever find them.

Some days I think of nothing but Nate
and his tenderness, his voice,
and I wonder why he doesn't call
and if we were together out of convenience
because we each needed someone, something.

Sitting on this rooftop
I am stoned and too high.

73

New York City towers above and around me —
trees below like twigs, cars like ants,
people specks of dust
and here I am on top of it all,
thinking about jumping twenty-eight floors
and making it all stop.
I am so close to the edge that I could vomit,
so close that it would be easy to jump.

All the windows are mirrors
and I imagine myself
covered in makeup, painted-on smile,
dyed hair for a highlight
on an otherwise gloomy face.

I am so high it's dizzying.
This world doesn't make sense.
Nothing makes sense.
Up here perspective is blurred.
Things I once thought were untouchable
look like they are in my reach.

I am lying down now, chin resting on the edge.
I cannot tell if this is a breakthrough

or a breakdown.
I'm too close to tell.
Too close.
Too high.

The more panic attacks I have
the harder it is to get back to normal.
If I have an attack
I feel defeated, sick, and fearful
that it will happen again.
I am on guard.
I move slowly.
I make excuses to not go out with friends.
I need to put as much distance
between me and the attack as possible.

In high school I could never remember what happened
when you added two negative numbers together.
My father once explained,
it's like riding an elevator farther down,
once you're already in the basement.
That's how I feel now —
stuck underground, and going deeper.

75

When kids make gross faces,
parents say, "One day
your face is going to stick like that."
I'm afraid that one day
my panic's going to stick
and it's going to be my entire life,
every second,
and there will be nothing else.

Being back at school for a new semester
makes me think that I can start over —
that things can be better.

Every night before dinner
Rebecca and her friends call me
to meet them at the dining hall.
I like knowing that I always have someone to sit with,
that on the weekends I am guaranteed a place
in Rebecca and Rachel's room
to get dressed before a party, watch movies,
do shots, or get stoned.

I am starting to feel things again.
I got my period today
and it is a gift.
The pain I am in is good.
The cramp in my uterus,
the blood, the aches, all good,
because I'd rather be in pain than be numb.

I can hear the birds in the distance.
I had forgotten what their voices sound like.
I can feel the sun on my face and legs.
I see bits of sopping green grass
poking out from the snow.
I smell spring, but only for a second.

Last year at this time
I was a senior in high school.
I had just finished my writing AP.
It was warm and beautiful
and I wonder if I was happy.

Today I feel unbelievably light.
For months I've been sick
from work and anxiety,

but now all of that is gone.
I have nothing to focus on —
no appointments, no deadlines,
and I don't know what to do
besides lie back on my bed.
I am left with a feeling
and I cannot tell if it's emptiness
or fullness.

V.

To celebrate the end of the year
all the girls take a road trip
to Jennifer's house in Vermont.
We pile into two cars
and sing Indigo Girls the whole way there.
Usually it is just Rebecca and me,
but now we are all together —
wandering the little town, cooking in Jennifer's kitchen,
packed into the bedrooms with sleeping bags.
I feel closer to them than before.

Ann, the girl Adam dated after me, is here
and at the end of the weekend
Rebecca and I drive back to school in her car.
She's timid, sweet, not as bad
as I thought she'd be.

My father is coming tomorrow
to pick me up and move me home.
Everything needs to be packed and ready to go
by the time he gets here at ten.
A row of garbage bags

79

filled with my crap lines the room.
The plastic tubs are stuffed and taped closed.

Sarah already left
and nothing is on the walls or shelves.
It looks like when I moved in,
only this time the space is familiar, lived in.

I can't believe this is it.
Tomorrow I go back
to live in my parents' house.

In my belly
I have a mild pushing pain,
or rather, an annoying pressure.
Not quite a throb, more of a twinge,
but more than a twinge.
Not quite pain, more like an uncomfortability.
Not sure exactly where, though.
Every time I try to pinpoint it,
it disappears.
I can't stand the mystery of it.
I hate the unknown and the ambiguous.

Sitting in the doctor's waiting room,
I wonder what has taken root in my belly.
Maybe it's a cyst on my ovaries.
I've heard they can grow to the size of a grapefruit.

The doctor looks like a grandfather
and I am embarrassed to have to spread my legs for him.
He pushes down on my belly from the outside,
reaches inside me and pushes up.
At the end of the exam
the doctor reports that I am fine.

Around two A.M. Nate is on top of me
and the phone is ringing.
Nate picks up and passes the phone to me.
It's my dad.
All he says is I better be home in ten minutes.
Nate makes a joke about not wanting to drive me home,
says my dad will be at the door with a shotgun.
At first I am scared of what my parents are going to say,
but by the time I get my clothes on I am furious.

My parents and I have the same fight we've had for years.
When I stay out late, it keeps my father up,

81

which keeps my mother up.
Then I have to hear from my mother
how tired it makes my father
and how he has to get up for work at six A.M.
I am eighteen.
What do they expect me to do?
To not go out?
To be home at midnight?

Why is it my fault if they can't sleep?
Plenty of parents manage to fall asleep
while their children are out of the house.
I can't live like this.
I will never live at home again.

I go upstairs and get ready for bed.
I wash my face,
take out my contacts,
put on my glasses,
and pick up my pills.
I've been taking Klonopin for more than six months.
I wonder if it still helps,
or if I have gotten better on my own,
or if it is a combination of the two.

Being with Nate is hard.
There is no accountability.
He pours himself into me —
tells me about his family, his fears,
how depressed he was before we knew each other.
He expects me to hold the weight
and then disappears for days.

I call Claire every morning
even though I know she's already left for work.
I like leaving her long messages
that she'll hear when she gets home.

Today Claire picks up after only two rings.
Everything she says sounds rehearsed.

"Joelle went into cardiac arrest yesterday afternoon.
Her boyfriend found her.
I woke up at 6:45 this morning,
the same time she died.
I just knew.
The doctors don't know why she died.
The police think she overdosed,
so they took her journals.

The doctors think it was meningitis
so they made us take some pills.
No one has any answers."

I ask her if she wants me
to come into the city right now.
She says, only if I need to.
I tell her, that's not the point,
Joelle was one of her best friends
and if she needs me now
I'll leave work and get on the next train.
I cannot believe that she is worried about my feelings.
I don't ask again.
I tell her I'm walking out the door
and will be there in forty minutes.

Walking to the train station,
I do not feel my feet hit the sidewalk.
It is just after noon and the sun is so strong
that there are sweat stains spreading under my arms.
Time isn't moving normally.
I feel like it takes forever to lift one foot off the ground,
bend my knee, and place my foot down again.

On the train, I sit with my cheek pressed against the cool
    window.
Long Island races past me, then Queens,
then the web of black cables that leads to the train yards.
When the train descends into the tunnels of Penn Station,
the windows become mirrors
and I can see how swollen and red my face is.

Days later, at the funeral,
Claire and I laugh through tears.
Joelle would have never worn the white ruffled blouse
and gold cross that her parents dressed her in.
Claire says this is not how she will remember Joelle.
Her face isn't the right shape or color.
But Claire insists that it's better this way —
that seeing Joelle like this will help her
accept that she is gone.

Claire speaks at the podium,
but I cannot hear her.
I see her mouth moving, but there are no words.
All I can think about is how blond her hair looks
against her black cotton dress.
Joelle's boyfriend is last to speak.

He says yesterday he went to Joelle's favorite restaurant
and ordered a bowl of chicken soup
for an empty seat.

All I want to do is sleep
and that makes me want to cry —
makes me remember how bad it was first semester,
when I hid under my blankets
in the darkness of drawn blinds.
I need sleep.
I need silence.
I need away.

I want to rest my head,
but I am afraid to sleep.
I am afraid I will wake up screaming.
I know it must be black under my eyes,
but it doesn't matter.
Things like my face do not matter.

This is different.
This is not panic.
This is sadness.
I can do this.
I will not get lost in the fog

because this is real.
Dying is real.

It is dark at the playground
and the only sounds are from the crickets.
The air is cooler than usual, moist.
I take my shoes off and swing.
Nate watches me from under the monkey bars.
I jump off, walk in the wet grass.
Nate puts his arms around me from behind,
kisses my neck, my shoulders.
My bare feet dig into the cold sand.
His hand touches my stomach,
under my tank top,
and I am electrified.
He lifts my shirt up,
exposes my chest to the cool air.
All the hairs on my body stand up
and I dig my feet deeper in the sand, ground myself.

Nate is work.
He is confused about everything —
especially his ex-girlfriend.

He thinks he still loves her
and because I love him
I say it's okay if he wants to go back to her.
Nate says he needs to take care of himself,
says he cannot deal with romance,
and a moment later his hand is reaching for my belt.
I want to do whatever I can for him.
I want to fix him, make him whole.
I want to teach him
that he doesn't have to fear people.
My actions are a lesson to him about love.

I crave broken men.
When I try to save other people
am I trying to save myself?
Am I covering up for my lack of strength
by putting people back together?
I am tired.
I want someone to save me —
build an intricate web
and place it beneath me in case I fall.

I feel better today.
I know that Nate cannot be
what I need him to be.
The waiting, the wanting,
and the desperation are familiar.
It is all too real, too soon.
My body cannot endure another Jason —
especially not this one, his best friend.

I've always wanted
to have my hair braided —
a whole head full of the long, skinny kind.
And after a summer of work, I have enough money
to go to one of those salons where only black women go.
I won't tell anyone how much it costs, though —
it's embarrassing that I would spend that much money,
but I want a change.
Rebecca goes with me to the salon,
sits down on the leather couch and waits
for eight hours as two women pull my hair and twist
in fake pieces so the braids will be longer, fuller.

When it's done and I walk out onto the street,
I feel people staring and it makes me uncomfortable.

Rebecca reminds me that I can't be upset.
"What did you expect?" she says.
"You're a skinny white girl
with a head of braids."

I'm not sure what my parents
thought I would look like,
but I can tell they hate it.
That they want me to look normal.

Part II

i.

Move-in day is like a sorority party.
Rebecca's friends and I are living in a suite.
Rebecca and Rachel and Amanda and Tara are in doubles,
Jennifer and I are in singles.
There is so much laughing
and loud music,
and running from room to room
to borrow a hammer or some tacks.

I love that I have my own room,
that I can do whatever I want to these walls.
I am committed to making this space mine.
I hang a giant tie-dyed tapestry over the back wall.
It's too bright, but I don't care.
My dad got me a futon and a rug
and this space looks good,
looks like me,
and I am the only one with a key.

Almost instantly the girls and I
establish ourselves as a unit —
we even call ourselves a herd.
We plan our days around each other,

meet for lunch,
walk to dinner at the same time,
go to the student center for coffee
late at night.

I think the best part
is when we sit together doing homework.
We don't need to talk.
It's just nice to be around people.

My anxiety is better,
but it's not great.
I've been taking Klonopin for almost a year
and my life has changed so much.
I have fewer panic attacks than freshman year,
but they are still there —
waiting for me
in the usual places.

The dining hall is still the worst.
The second I walk in the door
and swipe my ID,
a switch goes off in my mind.

As I walk around to find something to eat
or someone to sit with,
it feels like I am underwater.
My limbs are heavy.
Sounds are muffled.

This swimming feeling,
combined with the dim light of the dining hall,
makes me feel faint.
The thought of passing out
makes me start to panic,
makes me wonder if I have had enough to drink
or if I have eaten enough
so my body can function.

I imagine being on line to get some pasta,
my eyes rolling back in my head.
I can see myself passing out,
hitting the dirty tile floor with a thud
and waking up with a crowd of people standing above me,
thinking I am such a freak.

One by one the girls all learn
about my anxiety.

I don't need to come out and tell them —
all they need is to be in the right place
at the wrong time
and see it happen.

When Tara finds out
she says that it explains a lot —
that freshman year
I was distant
with everyone except Rebecca.
She would always see us
sitting in the dark, smoking,
writing in our journals.
She says that my unapproachability
and independence from the group
looked like maturity.
But now she says she understands
that I was that way
because I didn't work well in groups.
She says that now
she tries to get me one on one —
that I am better that way,
more focused.
It means so much to me
that she would go out of her way

to see me alone,
so she can get the best of me.

I have a dream
that I am walking in the woods
and I find a stone temple
with crumbling white pillars.

I am standing inside eating tuna fish
and realize there are tiny bones in it.
I stand over a basin
and start pulling wads of dry tuna fish
out of my mouth.
It is endless.
No matter how much tuna I scoop out
there is always more.

Nate and I talk,
but I am usually the one to call.
I hate that he does that,
but I have learned that I have two choices:
either accept it
or not be friends with him.

I stare at the phone,
start to dial,
and hang up.
I do this over and over.
I don't want to be the one to break first.
I don't want to be the one who needs him.
It makes me feel like he doesn't care —
that I am not as important to him
as he says I am.
But I always break.
I always call.
And when I do,
I forget
how hard it was to pick up the phone
when I hear his voice —
hear him say my name.

When we talk,
he likes to hear about school
and all the projects I am working on
and how well I am doing.
I think he looks up to me —
with my focus
and direction —
because he doesn't have that.

At lunch Ann sits down with me
and I am surprised
at how easy the conversation is.
She says how intimidated she was
by me and Rebecca that weekend at Jennifer's.
She says there was an impenetrable vibe about us,
but sitting here with me now,
she doesn't feel it.

It's weird to hear this again —
to hear how I was perceived
by people before they got to know me.
Some of the girls thought I was a bitch —
aloof, distant —
but now they see the truth.

The conversation shifts to guys
and I tell Ann
that Sean and I hooked up
a few weeks ago and she laughs.
She hooked up with him
at the very beginning of freshman year.
There is something about knowing this
that breaks a wall between us.

Just before Halloween,
Rebecca and I are at a party in town.
When things quiet down,
a few of us move upstairs
to another kid's apartment.
His name is Jeff
and I've never seen him before.
I would have remembered him.

When I bend down to look at his books,
he says Henry Miller is his favorite.
I smile and tell him mine is Anaïs Nin.
Henry Miller and Anaïs Nin were lovers.
We talk for a while about them.
I like the way this is starting —
with Henry and Anaïs.

I have the dream again,
this time with taffy.
I don't know where I am,
but it's like I'm a magician
pulling multicolored scarves out of my mouth
and the taffy won't stop coming.

100

Ann and I go to a party in town.
She drives us in her SUV
and seeing her sitting behind the wheel
makes her look even more petite.

The party is wall-to-wall people,
and even though it's cool outside
the apartment is warm and stuffy.
We find seats and watch people shuffle by
to find a drink or a friend.

Ann takes off her jacket
and then tugs at her turtleneck,
tries to give herself some air.
She pulls her blond hair off her neck
into a ponytail.
She looks uncomfortable,
but I figure it's because of the heat.

Some people I kind of know come by
and Ann barely says a word.
It's like she's not here.
Her green eyes grow wide
as she sinks lower and lower into the couch.

101

I lean over and ask if she's all right.
She shakes her head no.
Without a word she stands up and puts on her jacket.
She asks if I'll be able to find a ride home,
and when I say yes, she says she has to leave.
I tell her to wait, but she says she'll be okay.
She leaves before I can say anything else.
She doesn't look back.

I can't believe that I just watched
someone else have a panic attack.

Now I see Jeff on campus all the time.
Every time I turn around, there he is —
sitting on the green,
getting coffee at the student center,
walking through the English department.
He is like a ghost
who has materialized just for me.

The first time I go to Jeff's alone,
I stand at the door to his apartment, wait

to catch my breath
before I ring the bell
because I was too scared
to take the rickety elevator.

We talk for a long time.
It is one of those conversations
that should be awkward
but isn't,
and when we kiss
it is perfect —
except for the shaking.
It starts in my stomach
and goes to my legs
and teeth.
I shouldn't be cold.
Jeff is next to me,
on top of me,
under me.

Later, in bed, I peer over his head,
watch his cat claw at old issues of the *Times*
and then crawl into bed
over our legs.

And when I crawl
out of bed
to sleep on the floor
because he is a violent dreamer,
the cat takes my place beside him.

As I smoke
and sit with bare knees pressed to my chest,
the cat glares
between my legs,
and I wonder
if I didn't have the braids
would Jeff have ever noticed me?

As Ann and I get closer
to the dining hall for dinner,
I know I can't do it.
I can't go in.
I had a panic attack in Lit class in the afternoon
and I am tired.
My body can't take another one.
I can't go in there
with all that noise,
and the sounds of forks banging against plates,

and the hum of people,
and those dim lights.

Ann and I sit outside for a while.
She knows what it's like
and tries to calm me down.
She puts her hand on my back and rubs,
but I can't do it.
I feel weak for not being able to go in
and do something so simple, so normal,
but I am tired
and I just want to go home.

Since the night I saw her have a panic attack
things have been different.
She comes to me,
red-faced and crying,
to help her calm down.
I reassure her
that she's going to be okay,
that she's not going to die,
I feel her forehead, tell her she's cool,
and smooth down her fine blond hair.

She does the same for me.
She becomes the voice of reason
when there is none.
When I feel myself on the edge
and I don't know what else to do,
I call her.

We do for each other
what we cannot do for ourselves.
When it is happening we are in another place
where the rules of reason do not apply.
We need a voice from the outside
because our own voices cannot be trusted.

We met too late,
or maybe too early.
Jeff's graduating
at the end of this semester.

There are so many things about him
that scare me,
but I cannot lose another chance to fear —
fear of being vulnerable,
fear of being hurt —

when all this time I've been hurting myself.
Putting the potential for damage
into someone else's hands is scary.
I have to have control,
even if it is the power to self-destruct.

Jeff scares me because he is smart,
because maybe I won't understand
or maybe because he'll make me stand up taller.
I'm scared of what will happen
when he leaves in two months,
and it's only been a week and a day.

I want things so bad
that I force them,
push them until they tear.

Snow again.
Every time the seasons change
I think about the year before.
I wonder how I felt
and if I thought the snow was as beautiful
as it is right now.

I have the dream again,
this time with glass.
I am standing near an ice sculpture
that is starting to melt.
My mouth is filled with glass
and I am bleeding and drooling all over myself.
I keep spitting out tiny shards,
but it is never enough.

Jeff and I are going to a play
at a tiny theater in town.
I've bought a bottle of wine
for afterwards.
When I get to his apartment to meet him,
he isn't there.
I call him over and over
from a pay phone outside.
It is raining and this feels like Jason.
For every minute I wait,
my anger builds.
For every time the bottle of wine clangs
against the stuff in my bag,
I hate him.

He finally comes downstairs,
apologizes,
says he was watching *Seinfeld* at his neighbor's,
and we walk to the play in silence.

The play is bizarre
and there are dead baby dolls
hanging from the ceiling.

Back at his apartment,
before I have a chance
to open the wine,
he tells me it'd be better
if we didn't see each other
since he's graduating
and then traveling in Europe.
He says it's only going to get harder.
But I don't feel any better.
It doesn't feel any easier.
And I can't believe
that it is happening again —
that I have found something good
only to have it taken away.

We have an awkward good-bye hug
as I wait for Rachel and Rebecca to pick me up.
He kisses me on the forehead
right between my eyes —
as if I didn't feel bad enough.

This night was supposed to be fun —
a bottle of wine
and me staying over,
but now I am sitting on a bench
behind the dorms with Rebecca
and I am crying.
There is a pit in my stomach
and I plan to fill it with wine.
Half a bottle later,
I am in my room, cutting my braids out.
I know I am drunk.
I know I am being dramatic,
but it feels good.

In the morning I don't go to class.
I go to breakfast so late
they are already clearing for lunch.
When I get my cereal,
I see a ghost.

There he is,
in the dining hall,
and I have never seen him here before.
We both smile
and he sits down with me.
He asks how I am
and I tell him about the bottle
meant for us
and the braids.
And it doesn't hurt to see him
like I thought it would.

ii.

I am home for winter break
and I can't tell if things have gone back to normal,
or if this part of my life is the anomaly.
Things are how they were
just before I left for school last year.
I spend most of my days working at the theater
trying to earn some cash.
I sit in the booth and sell tickets
to rich people who think I'm retarded.
Men hit on me,
say, "You're such a pretty girl.
Why don't you smile?"
I'm in a tiny glass booth
making seven dollars an hour.
What do I have to smile about?
Usually I just bare my teeth
like an animal in response.

I try to entertain myself in the booth
so I don't go crazy.
When it's quiet
I do crosswords and read.
When it's busy

and a customer is being rude
and paying with a fifty or a hundred,
I pull out the yellow marker
to see if the bill is real.
It drives men nuts
and makes me laugh.

At home it's the usual drill.
My parents are constantly on top of me.
They want to know where I'm going,
and when I'll be back.

I try not to stay out too late
and dodge the same fight we always have
about how it keeps my father up.
When I am out with friends
I constantly check my watch
and feel guilty
that me being out with my friends
affects my parents.
But it also makes me angry.
I am always the first to leave
and none of my friends understand why.

It's the end of winter break
and I feel sick.
My head is heavy, stuffed with snot,
and my joints ache.
When I tell my parents I am going to Nate's house,
my mother protests, says I am sick
and shouldn't be going anywhere,
but I convince my father otherwise.
It's my last night at home
and I want to see Nate.

When I get to his house, Jason is there
and I wonder if they are as uncomfortable as I am.
The three of us smoke a joint
and I fall asleep on Nate's couch
as they watch basketball.

The next morning I am worse than before.
I shuffle out of bed to the kitchen
    to find some decongestants.
My father is cooking, and the TV is on loud.
I sit down in the dining room.
I don't have the strength to take the pills.
I brace my elbows on my knees
and hang my head down.

114

I feel like I am being crushed.
My head is sinking lower and lower
and then everything flips.
I have no sense of up or down, only suspension.
I want to call to my father, but I can't.
My sister walks through the room,
asks me how I'm feeling,
and all I can do is reach out my hand.
She tries to get me to the living room to lie down,
but we don't make it.

I wake up on the floor by the front door.
Something wet is on my head
and my father is bent over me,
kissing my face, over and over.

The fire trucks come first,
then the ambulance.
The foyer is filled with people.
I try to tell them I feel better,
but everyone insists I go to the hospital.
The EMTs won't let me walk to the ambulance.
They have to take me on a stretcher.
Up I go, strapped in,

carried out of my house
with all the neighbors watching.

Back at school,
my therapist and I talk about passing out.
I tell her it is terrifying to be lost
somewhere in between here and there
in the dark nothingness,
to have moments of time
unaccounted for.

Passing out makes me think about death —
about the moment before dying
and how it must feel
to be pulled away from everything you love
and have no control.

I tell her about winter break
and the ambulance and the high fever
and how I spent the day in the hospital,
hooked up to an IV and getting tested for everything.
I tell her it's not the first time I passed out.
The first time was when I was fifteen.
My sister took me to a concert in the city.

We were up front by the stage, next to the speakers.
The bass was crushing my chest.
I was light-headed and then things began to fade.
The night sky flashed in front of my eyes
and the floor caved in.

My sister's friend carried me outside
and sat me down in the cool air.
My hands were vibrating.
I asked my sister if she could feel it,
but she couldn't.
I could see how much it scared her
to not feel what I was feeling.

The next summer it happened again
at an outdoor concert with Abe and Matt.
We were packed in, body to body,
trying to get to the small gate in the fence.
I was overwhelmed by all the people, the noise,
and then things began to fade.
I reached out for Abe,
but before I could say anything,
I fell backwards into the crowd.

I woke up with Abe over me
and I was embarrassed at all the drama.
Medics came rushing into the crowd
and cut a hole open in the fence to get me out.

Later that summer I was in a bar
and I got a bloody nose from the heat.
Once my friends realized what was wrong
they all piled into the bathroom.
They tried to give me advice
on how to make the bleeding stop
and I passed out.

I came to as I was being carried to the street.
When the ambulance came,
they had to take me to the hospital
and call my parents because I was a minor.
The biggest problem I could see was
that I had lied to my parents about where I was
and it was two-thirty in the morning.

iii.

It is a new semester.
Everything is hidden
under the snow.
In my advisor's office
I am talking about credits
and fulfilling requirements
when I look out the window
at the parking lot and the woods,
and there, carrying a box,
wearing a jacket that is too thin,
is Jeff.
I grab my stuff
and tell my advisor that I've got to go —
that I've seen a ghost.
I go down the stairs two at a time,
past the Education Department,
and out the side door.
I don't even put on my jacket.
I catch up to him as he is getting in the driver's seat.
He says his trip got delayed
and now he's finally finished packing up his stuff
and heading back to the city.
I can't believe that he's been here all this time,

119

that I never knew,
that he never called.

Valentine's Day is shit.
It makes me remember elementary school
and how we made cards out of doilies and glitter.
The teacher would staple little mailbox pouches to the wall
and carefully print our names on them.
Somehow I never got as many notes as the other girls.

The only person I can think about is Nate
and how I wish things were different.
I want to send him something.
I want to do something special for him,
but nothing seems right —
everything seems too big.
Finally I settle on sending him one Hershey's Kiss.
I feel good.
This is good.
It is the right thing.

My therapist says I am better.
My psychiatrist says I am better.
I think I am better.

I am counting down the days
until I finish tapering off my meds.
The bottle of pills is nearly empty.

Five yellow pills,
bits of confetti
that have settled
after a party.

Four yellow pills,
lined up in a T.

Three yellow pills,
a miniature pyramid.

Two yellow pills,
jaundiced eyes staring at me.

One yellow pill left
and it is the best
and scariest feeling.

I am nervous about life
without medication.
It's a catch-22
to take someone with anxiety disorder
off medication.
Just knowing that I won't have it in my bag
or in my blood makes me anxious.
I wish there were some way to take me off it
without telling me.

I wonder
if things really have changed,
or if it is the pills.
I feel strong
for doing this,
but it makes me wonder
if I am dependent, weak.
I have so many conflicting emotions.
I am scared,
but mostly proud.

There's this guy in my poetry class
who is amazing.
I dream about him almost every night.

Walking to class one day I tell him
he was in my dream last night
and he smiles like it's good news.

A few days later I see him in a bar
and we talk about dreaming.
He wishes he could remember his dreams.
I tell him about how I keep a dream journal
and how when you first wake up,
you can't let yourself think about anything
besides what you were dreaming.

Days later, we hang out late after a party.
It is nearly five and we stop at the gas station
so he can buy cigarettes and I can buy a lotto ticket.
I am feeling lucky.
The ticket machine isn't on yet
so we wait and walk through the aisles.
He buys me a red Ring Pop and I think
it's the best thing anyone's ever given me.

At his apartment he asks how the Ring Pop tastes
and when I say, "It tastes red,"
he smiles and kisses me
to see for himself.

I can't stop shaking as we make out.
I ask him if he can feel it
and when he says no, I am surprised.
To cover up for how crazy I am,
I tell him I am cold
and we take a hot shower
and come back and pile on the blankets,
but that doesn't help either.

iv.

I promised myself that I wouldn't live at home again
so I am going to live with Claire
and her parents in the city for the summer.
I have a job working at the same office as my sister
and it's just a few blocks from Claire's house.
My only responsibility
is to earn money to go to Paris next spring.

Work sucks.
I am the token somewhat-blond
receptionist at the door.
I work nine to five,
have lunch with Audrey and my sister every day,
do busywork at my desk,
and calculate how long it will take
to earn money for Paris.

One afternoon
my boss calls me into his office
to tell me that my skirt is too short.
He doesn't say it
and then let it go.
He goes on and on.

I try to end the conversation,
but he won't let it drop.
On my way out of his office
he reaches into his desk
and pulls out German chocolates
wrapped in colored foil.

Now if I come into the office in the morning
and do not go directly to his office
he calls me at my desk
and asks why I haven't come to say hello.

In his office one afternoon,
he tells me he took one of my coworkers out for dinner,
that he does that with his staff from time to time.
He asks if I would like to go to dinner
and I say yes, without thinking.
But as the word comes out of my mouth,
I wish I could take it back.
As he hands me chocolates, I wonder
if he's ever asked my sister to dinner
or given her chocolates.

Later in the week
he asks when we should go to dinner.

I try to maneuver around the subject.
He asks where we should go.
I feel trapped.
How could I go out with him?
I'm nineteen and he's in his fifties.
What would we talk about? Golf?
I don't even know what to say
to my father when we have dinner alone.

I can't stop thinking about it
and he won't let it drop.
He asks me nearly every day.
I never wear skirts anymore —
no matter what length —
and my stomach knots
every day before work.
Now when he gives me chocolates
I throw them out.

I ask my new therapist
how I can make him stop
and she says to tell him I thought about it
and that it makes me uncomfortable.
She emphasizes the word uncomfortable.

She says if a manager hears that word,
he'll get the point and back off.

In his office the next day,
I tell him what I have rehearsed,
but it doesn't work.
He wants to know why I changed my mind.
I tell him that when he asked,
I spoke too quickly,
and that I was sorry,
but I thought about it
and it makes me *uncomfortable*.
Maybe he missed that word the first time
so I say it again.

Now instead of asking me out every day,
he wants to know who I talked to,
who changed my mind.
I have headaches every day,
my stomach is always upset,
and all I can think about is my sister
and how I feel guilty
for getting the attention.

I barely see Nate this summer.
I visit him a few times downtown
while he paints.
We talk about how he's going to Spain
for the fall semester
and he shows me a painting he did
and points to this one part,
a bridge, and tells me he thought of me
when he painted it.
It is so sad
how knowing something
so small
can make me so happy.

New York City skyline
at night, twenty-seven floors up.
In my head I can hear it like a chant,
like a dare.
Jump.
Jump.
Jump.

I don't want to jump,
but I feel like my body will betray me

129

and I will swing my legs over the balcony railing
and push myself onto First Avenue.

I cannot trust this body,
or maybe this is what I really want.
Maybe this is the truth.

Backed up against the brick wall,
I hold on to the handle of the sliding door
with one hand and trace the space
in between the rectangles with the other.

I run inside the apartment,
slam the door shut, and get into bed.

The bathroom light is on
and the door is open.
I hear it again, stronger.
You will get up and put your head in the toilet.
What will my parents think in the morning
when I'm found dead,
head in the bowl?

In my head I hear, *This is not a choice.*
I tell myself over and over,

130

I am stronger than you,
stronger than you,
stronger than you.

I get out of bed and run to the bathroom.
I switch off the light
and lock the door from the outside.
I am stronger than this,
than you,
than what you think I am.

This is not real.
Not real.
Not real.

I am scared of myself,
I tell my therapist.
I tell her what happened on the balcony
and how I felt like I was at war
with my body.
I don't think
I want to kill myself, I say.
She tells me this is common
for people who have anxiety disorder.

It's good to know
that I'm not the only unsuicidal person
thinking about killing herself.

I see Jason
for the first time
in a long time.
We go swimming
and dive around each other
like curious fish.
The lifeguard watches us and smiles.
Jason picks me up and throws me around.
Where it's too deep for me to stand
I put my arms around Jason's neck
and my legs around his waist.
Our bodies are still a perfect fit.

There is too much movement.
I bring my stuff from Claire's apartment
to my parents' house.
I get a fresh box of garbage bags
and pull out the plastic bins.
It's time to pack up again.

132

Part III

i.

Rebecca and I make a pact.
Since this semester Ann is in England,
Rachel is in Italy,
Tara is in Australia,
and Jennifer is in France,
we are determined
to make new friends.

My first new friend is going to be Robyn.
She and I met last semester
while she was showing her new tattoo
to some friends we had in common.
We started talking
and I showed her my poetry.
She loved it and said
she wanted to turn one of my poems
into a book for one of her design classes.

At the beginning of the semester
Robyn makes good on her promise.
She wants to know
which poem she can have.
I give her a few to choose from

and she picks one about
going to Jeff's apartment for the first time.
She tells me she wants me to give input about layout
and even wants to take photos of me
to illustrate the book.

On Thursday afternoon
when neither of us has classes,
we pack up her camera and props
and go into town to Jeff's building.
Robyn wants to take photos of me
in the elevator and on the stairs.
I'm a little nervous.
That guy from my poetry class
lives in this building too,
and I haven't spoken to him
since we hooked up.
What if he sees me?
He'll think I'm a stalker.

Robyn and I laugh.
We feel like we are on a covert mission
as we sneak into the building.
Every time we hear someone
on the stairs or calling the elevator

I cringe.
When we finish I can't get away
from the building fast enough.
But it's fun being with her
and playing like little kids.

Things are good this semester.
I've been off medication since last spring
and my life has mostly gone back to normal.
I haven't seen the inside
of a therapist's office in months.
Most of the time I just daydream
about going to Paris with Rebecca
and how it's going to be.
I think about all the countries I am going to see
and how romantic it will be to wander new streets.

I'm tired of how repetitive things are here.

Jason comes to visit
and I'm not sure if it's to see me
or his other friend who goes to school here.

Robyn and I go to a party with Jason
where his other friend will be.
It's not a crowd I would hang out with
if he weren't here.

At the party, Robyn and I wander around the house
as Jason makes friends
with everyone in the room.
Robyn and I go upstairs
and before I can even take a seat,
Robyn is gone.

I find her outside on the porch.
I ask what's going on,
and she says she needs to leave.
I don't understand.
She says that when we walked upstairs
she saw a guy she has a crush on doing coke.
She's crying,
and I don't understand.
Her reaction is too intense.
She says that a year ago
a friend of hers was really depressed,
got into coke,
and killed himself.

She says she can't be here.
I flip into action mode.
If she needs to leave,
then we will leave right then
and walk the mile back to campus.
Part of me doesn't want to leave Jason.
I never get to see him, but this is more important.
I find Jason, tell him we're leaving,
and tell him to call me
when he wants to come back to my room
for the night.

Robyn and I are walking,
arms around each other,
and she tells me about her friend.
I try to get her to think about happy times
they had together and she calms down
a little.

We only get a few blocks
when we hear Jason behind us.
As the three of us walk back to campus
we pass a giant pile of leaves.
It is calling to be played in.

Jason dives in first,
then Robyn,
then me.
The leaves smell amazing,
dried and smoky.
We look like little kids
as we swim around
and toss leaves at each other.
I can't remember the last time I was this happy.

Jason and I drop Robyn at her dorm
and go back to my room.
This is it.
We haven't talked about it,
but it's hard to imagine we won't hook up.
After all these years
this will only be the third time
we've spent the night together.
When I change for bed,
I just turn around,
let him watch me.

We get into the twin bed,
and I feel like I am sixteen again.
Jason picks a bit of a leaf out of my hair

and that starts us kissing
Kissing him is like kissing myself.
He was my first boyfriend —
I learned to kiss from him.
He tastes the same as he did
two and a half years ago.
His body is different, though.
There's more muscle,
more strength.

We fall asleep for a while
and when I wake up
I look at him sleeping
and just smile.
A spell has been broken.

ii.

Four months go by quickly.
Everything I do
is just another milestone
that gets me closer to Paris.

Like always, the snow comes
before Halloween,
then there's Thanksgiving,
and final exams,
and then I am packing to go home,
and packing again for Paris.

I feel like Paris is going to mark the start
of a new chapter for me.
My anxiety has been at bay for months
and I finally feel far enough away from it
to gain perspective
on everything that's happened to me
and everything I've done.

Rebecca and I
are in the airport with our parents.

It's overwhelming
to have them here waiting with us.

At first the flight is delayed
two hours because of bad weather.
When we finally board
we end up sitting on the runway
for several more hours
because the plane needs to be de-iced.
Rebecca and I pass the time
by attempting to speak broken French.

When we are finally ready to go,
a voice comes over the loudspeaker.
The plane is delayed again.
The pilot is sick and needs to be taken off board.
I just want to get there.
We finally take off at the same time
we should have landed in Paris.

In the hotel in Paris
the night before our host families pick us up,
everything is surreal.

143

I open the long windows in my room
and look out.
The street below is narrow
and the way the light hits
the buildings across the street
makes them look flat,
like part of a movie set.

In the morning Rebecca and I wait
in the lobby with all the other students.
We are like puppies
hoping to be given a good home.

When my name is called,
there is a tiny woman waiting for me.
I am scared that I won't understand
the very first thing she says to me,
even though I have taken three semesters of French
and have been practicing
basic phrases all morning.
I turn back to Rebecca
and mouth *au revoir.*
We smile nervously at each other.
I know we are both praying
our families will be nice.

The coordinator introduces me to my host mother.
Her name is Laurence and I am horrified
to learn that she speaks no English.

Laurence and I take a taxi home
and it is sweet how she speaks slowly to me.
She needs to repeat nearly everything she says,
and even then I only understand every few words.
I am embarrassed by my accent
and how I stammer out broken sentences,
but she just smiles at me.

She tells me about her kids.
From what I can make out, there are three,
but I can't tell how many are sons
and how many are daughters.
The words *fille* and *fils* sound too similar.

This surge of energy
and excitement is amazing.
I can't wait to see my new home
and meet the rest of the family.
I feel like at any moment
I could start jumping up and down
and clapping my hands like a little kid.

145

When we get to the apartment building
she directs me into a tiny elevator.
I barely fit inside with my suitcase
while she takes the stairs.
We meet on the fourth floor
and she leads me inside.
The apartment is beautiful
in a shabby sort of way.
She shows me my room first.
It has a fresh coat of yellow paint
and is filled with light
coming in from those long windows
that look like doors.
There is a view of a courtyard
and looking down makes me feel
like I have gone back in time.

I am in the sixth arrondissement, on the Left Bank.
This neighborhood is chic,
with high-end clothing stores on my block
like Yves Saint Laurent and Miu Miu.
As Laurence and I walk around the neighborhood
she shows me all the little shops:
the bakery just downstairs,
the cheese shop, the butcher shop.

It is adorable how each type of food
has its own store.
My body is exhausted from the flight,
but inside I am buzzing.

Later in the day,
her two sons come home.
Augustin is thirteen and Alexis is sixteen
and I finally understand
what Laurence was trying to tell me about Alexis.
He is handicapped.
He has a prosthetic hand
and a blank look on his face.

When the boys are not staring at me,
they are talking fast, not enunciating,
and using so much slang that it is useless
to try to understand them.

I am surprised at how calm I am
while I sit in a room
with complete strangers
speaking a different language
and all I can manage to say is *quoi?* and *oui,*
like a parrot with poor vocabulary.

147

That night I meet Laurence's daughter.
Phyllis is only a few years older than me
and she speaks nearly fluent English.
Knowing that she'll be around to help me
is such a relief.

Nate and I talked today.
He's been in Spain since the fall semester.
We talked for a long time
about how being out of our neighborhood
and away from his family has changed him.
He's opening up
and learning to be himself.

Nate will only be in Spain for one more week
and all I want to do is go and see him.
If I don't see him now,
I won't see him for another five months.
But it's too soon.
There are too many things happening in Paris
and I'm not even sure he wants me there.

Rebecca and I
and a few other girls
are shopping near my apartment.
It's colder now that the sun has set
and I leave them in a café
to go home and get a heavier jacket.

On my way home
I take a wrong turn and get lost.
I ask people where rue du Cherche-Midi is.
I know I can't be more than a few blocks away,
but no one knows.
How could no one know where it is?
Is it my accent?
Am I not making any sense?

I go into a men's clothing store.
I am nearly in tears.
I say,
very simply
and with my best accent,
that I am lost,
that I am looking for rue du Cherche-Midi.
They put up their hands
and tell me how sorry they are.

149

I haven't managed to memorize
my family's eight-digit telephone number
so I can't even call someone to come and get me.
I will not cry on the streets of Paris.
I will not cry.
I will not cry.

I have started to settle into my new routine.
I don't feel like a tourist.
There is no time.
I am taking classes in French language and culture
and teaching English conversation at a high school.
On Wednesdays I get to be an artist.
I put on ratty jeans and take the metro
to the western edge of the city
for a photography class in the morning
and then go to the eastern edge
for painting in the afternoon.
The metro that connects the two
stays aboveground most of the way
and it is the longest
and most beautiful commute I have ever had.

I have had very little anxiety and panic
because the fear is real.
I feel dumb
because I cannot express myself in words.
I've become mute.
If I stop paying attention for even a second,
I lose all understanding.

I am so easily frustrated here —
like when I was little
and my dad tried to help me with math.
All I wanted to do was scream,
jump out of my skin
and away from the kitchen table,
but taking photos
and exploring the city by myself
makes me feel human —
makes me feel calm.
My photos let me show other people how I see.
That's all I ever wanted.

Painting class is not going well.
I look up at the model,

151

hold up my paintbrush to get the proportions,
and try to paint her on the page,
but I can't get my hand to create
what I see in front of me.
My portrait makes this beautiful woman
look orange and lumpy.

On the metro going home,
all I can think about is
how what I create and what I do
is not good enough.
I turn up my CD player loud
for the first time in a long time.
I could never do this before.
The idea of blocking out
all other sounds has always been scary.
It makes my heart race,
makes me feel like I can't breathe,
but today I crank it up
and want to cry
because this is not easy
and this is the first work
I have done in years.

I have decided that it is time
to do something drastic.
I am going to get a real French haircut.

Sitting in the chair,
the stylist inspects my face.
He checks me out from all angles
and then gestures how short he is going to cut —
at least five inches from the front
and even more from the back.
I'm scared, but I need this
weight off of me.

I miss home
or at least being able to go home.
Looking at photos makes me want to cry.
I sit in my room,
staring at the phone,
not knowing who to call.
I've already forgotten the numbers.

I have become an introvert
because I don't have a large enough vocabulary
to be anything else.

Locked inside my head, my body,
all I do is think
and it is making me well.

I am trying to find myself
in all of the chaos,
find something that I can call me
inside the screams and inside
the *you should*s and *you have to be*s.

I am grown in so many ways,
but in front of my parents
I am still a child.
I am having a hard time throwing off the skin
that I pick and peel.
I am the only one who can do it,
but I can't seem to let myself.

I am getting so healthy here.
I can close my eyes on the metro
and let the speed move me —
another thing I could never do before.

I have found my body
and come to terms with the space it takes up.
I am confident enough to know
that even when there is only blackness around me
and voices with no mouths —
that I still remain.
Before, I disappeared.

I have found a comfortable space —
five feet six inches,
one hundred and thirty pounds,
with long fingers and toes,
small breasts,
and I like what I see.

Progress, baby steps.
I feel like I am checking things off a list,
but instead of accomplishing feats
like skydiving or swimming with sharks,
I am listening to my CD player on high in public
and keeping my eyes shut around other people.
It seems crazy to be proud of these things,
but I am.

Living with Laurence and her family
is a lot like living with my parents.
I wake up to the sounds of screaming and fighting.
When Rebecca sleeps over,
she doesn't understand how I deal with it.

I feel like a member of their family.
I watch cartoons with Augustin
when he gets home from school.
I drink wine and smoke
with Laurence as she cooks dinner.
I go to parties with Phyllis
and her friends.
And then there is Alexis.
He has the maturity of a six-year-old
and is obsessed with James Dean and Elvis Presley.
He has to be told when to eat
and when to shower.
He is anxious around people,
especially women,
and does not realize that when he stares
he makes people nervous.
I have infinite patience with him
as he shows me his collection
of James Dean memorabilia

156

and asks me to translate Elvis songs.
I spend hours helping him
with his math homework.
Laurence is amazed at the progress we make
and jokes that she is going to fire his tutor.

The city has been wet and gray since I got here.
Finally seeing the sun
and sitting in the Luxembourg Gardens
makes such a big difference.
Being outside is a pleasure.
In the sun I can see myself.
I don't know when I have felt this calm.
It's the sun
and the fact that I stayed on the metro
five extra stops
just to hear a man playing the drums.

I get so much smaller when I am in a city.
I remember the first time
I realized that I wasn't the only person who cried.
I was in the car, pulled up to a red light.
Maybe I was crying, or one of my parents was yelling,
or maybe I was just staring out the window,

but in the backseat of the car next to us
was a little girl crying.

All of a sudden the world opened up
and it's doing it again now.
In this garden there are so many stories,
so many other problems besides mine.

I am jealous of the little kid
spinning around near the fountain.
What would these people think
if I were to start spinning
with my arms spread wide?
Regardez, elle est complètement folle!
A lunatic on drugs, probably.
My greatest accomplishment here is not caring,
letting go of other people's opinions.
I am not wound as tight.
I can let go,
just no spinning yet.

Everyone is all smiles
and kisses today in the park.
I am in the corner with my journal and CD player
just loud enough to hear the water

158

coming from the fountain and a few muffled voices
speaking another language.
I could stay in the Luxembourg Gardens forever
if I had the right person next to me
for conversation.
Even the pigeons are dancing, kissing,
going in circles, mounting each other.
Paris is the city of love,
even for the birds.

iii.

All of the students in our program
go to Provence for the weekend.
After a day of sightseeing
we are at our hotel,
sitting around rough wooden tables,
drinking wine and laughing,
when I feel panic surge through my body.
My breathing gets off track
and when I ask for water,
I know I am in trouble.
That's the first sign
that this is not going to get better.

My eyes are darting around the room
wondering who can tell that I am freaking out
and just like that, I need to leave.
It doesn't matter
that they haven't served dinner yet.
It doesn't matter
that I was sitting with my friends.
All that matters is that I have to get out
to make this stop.

I tell everyone that I am tired
and go back to my room.
I try getting into bed and falling asleep,
but that doesn't work.
I am too frantic.
There is no TV, no radio,
nothing to distract me.
I am freezing cold
even though the weather is pleasant.

I take a hot shower
to take away the chill
and calm the creeping feeling
that is going through my chest.
I sit on the shower floor
and let the water pour over me
as I rock back and forth, crying,
staring at the tiles on the wall
and wondering what I did to deserve this.

The steam makes me feel like I am choking
and I am worried that the bathroom door is locked
and if I die in the shower,
no one will be able to get to me.
I cannot do this alone.

161

I cannot die alone.
I must swallow any pride I have left,
put on clothes and shoes,
and get the one person
I can cry in front of,
the one person who will leave anywhere
on a moment's notice
because she knows.

I gather myself up
and head out the door.
It's too dark
and I hate this place.
I hate being here
and there she is,
having fun,
talking, drinking, eating,
having a life —
a normal life.
Rebecca looks beautiful and normal
and I am going to interrupt that.
I lean down and whisper in her ear.
I try not to look at anyone else
in case they get a glimpse
of how insane I am.

162

She puts down her napkin.
And that is it.
No questions.
She's done this before
and we both know
she'll do it again.

I cannot stop crying and shaking.
Rebecca wants to know what to do for me.
I tell her I feel like I can't breathe,
so we walk outside, down a path
with perfectly manicured hedges.
I feel like I can't control my limbs
and the sound inside my head is like a tornado.
I want to cover my ears,
but I know the sound is deep inside.

I have a moment of clarity
as we are walking.
For the first time I understand
the concept of suicide.
I can understand the feeling
of wanting *it* to stop
and being willing to do

whatever it takes
to make sure that happens.

We go back to our room
and Rebecca gets into bed with me.
I ask her to distract me,
so she tells me stories
about people she grew up with.
She even gets me to laugh a little.
Hearing her voice —
hearing something besides the thoughts
ripping through my mind —
is calming.

I just need to put a little space
between me and the panic.
I need a little bit of calm
so I can get a grip
and hold on to something,
to pull myself up
and out.

The next morning,
I am as tired as if I hadn't slept.
I feel hungover and stiff.

The entire day I am walking a fine line
between normal and crazy.
I drink water constantly
to make sure I won't pass out.
The day goes reasonably well
until dinner.
Our group is on the bus, pulling up to a restaurant
when the electricity races up my chest
and stops with a fizzle at my lips.

I cannot go in there.
I cannot sit down
and act normal
over a leisurely dinner.
It is not possible.
Everyone gets off the bus
and I tell Rebecca
I cannot go in there.
I need to walk.
I need to move.
I cannot sit.
I cannot be confined.

We walk down the road a little
and there is nothing

165

but fields on all sides.
Just the restaurant and our bus and some fields
and I am babbling like a lunatic,
wishing I could take off running
and never come back.
This is it, I think.
I have finally gone completely insane.

After a few minutes of walking
I tell Rebecca she has to go get our coordinator.
I need to go to a hospital
because
I
can
not
do
this.

The only thing that makes me feel better
is the thought of slightly stiff hospital sheets,
the scent of disinfectant,
and a tag on my wrist
with my name and information.

Our coordinator comes out
and wants to know what is going on.
I wonder if he has been trained for this,
if he got a pamphlet
titled, *What to do if one of your students
goes insane on a back road in the middle of nowhere.*
He tries to coax me inside,
but I am not ready for that.
He tells me that he used to have panic attacks,
but they went away,
just like that.
One day, he grew out of them.
His anecdote converts some of my panic
into anger.

His story insults me,
makes me feel as if what I am going through
is not significant —
that it's just a phase.

His wife comes out
and suggests that I have some wine,
that it will help relax me.
She says she has some pills
at the hotel she can give me.

167

This is what I want to hear.
I want solutions.

The restaurant sets up a table for me and Rebecca
away from the others
because there is no way
I can be around that many people
staring at me and thinking I am insane.

The next day we are supposed to tour Avignon,
but I cannot go with the group.
It is too dangerous.
I need to keep myself safe.
Another girl is sitting out the day too.
From what she says,
it sounds like she has irritable bowel syndrome
and it's nice to know
that I am in good company.

We stay at a café
while the others walk around.
There is a table with a man and his son.
Over and over the son asks, *"C'est quoi ça?"*
To be that young

and not know what things are
is enviable.

She and I sit outside in the sun in the town square.
I reassure myself that I have eaten enough,
that I won't pass out,
but I wonder if I have had enough water.
Always the fear of the uncontrollable
dark times when I am somewhere
in between here and there.

I feel safer being with her,
but my body is still buzzing
and at any moment
I could have another panic attack.

I know I am sick,
I just thought I was better.

It is over
and I am back in Paris and I am tired
as if I have been in a war.
My stomach is still clenched
and I don't know when it will let go.

169

I feel like I am back at square one,
at the edge of something,
and I don't know what will be there when I fall.
Two days ago I was willing to commit myself
and now all is calm,
but the old fears have come back
and I could break at any minute.

I wonder how I must look
to Rebecca when it happens.
It's scarier than physical illness
because there is no vomit or fever.
Nothing external.
Nothing to see
but the fear in my eyes
and it scares me
because I don't know what to do anymore.
I don't have any answers
and so many times this weekend
I had to ask for Rebecca's help.

This hurts
more than anything else
because I cannot stop it.

"Here's the thing, Doctor,
I have a history of anxiety disorder.
I've been off meds for almost a year and a half,
but now things are bad, really bad,
and I can feel they are going to get worse.
I need something.
Spring break is coming up soon
and I couldn't even handle a weekend in the countryside.
I've got plans, three countries in two weeks.
I've got tickets and made promises to my friend,
so I need you to prescribe something to chill me out
because I know it is coming
and I need to be ready."

Lexomyl 6 mg
looks like a tiny row of teeth
and can be broken into four pieces.
I swallow one miniature tooth after another
until I can fall asleep.

SAM-e 200 mg
is a supplement
and looks like a fat brown M&M.

The doctor says it is all natural
and I don't believe for a second
that it is going to make a difference.

iv.

Rebecca and I are in Florence with Robyn.
We have two weeks of spring break ahead of us.
We are armed with Eurail passes,
giant backpacks, a list of hostels,
and a bottle of sedatives.

First Florence, Venice, and Rome,
then a train from Rome to the south of France,
an overnight train from Nice to Barcelona,
and possibly south in Spain.

Rebecca and I are a good team.
She doesn't care enough to do research
and I'm a control freak.
I have our trip planned out.
Nearly every day is accounted for.

I'm nervous to go
after what happened in Provence,
but we made all these plans
and there are so many places I want to see.
Knowing that I have pills in my backpack
makes me feel safer.

On the way to Robyn's favorite restaurant,
the panic hits and I start crying quiet, slow tears
because I do not have the strength to do this again.
We are walking up a cobblestone street
and I look over at Rebecca and shake my head,
hang it low.

Some people love dusk —
the blue-gray cloud
that covers everything.
It makes my eyes roll back in my head,
makes my head swim.
It makes me cold.

At the restaurant
we order the tasting menu.
Slowly, plate after plate,
the food comes.
I feel crushed by time.
I don't see how I can make it
through all the courses
without screaming.
My stomach is cramped.
I am going to be sick.

In the bathroom
I assume the familiar position —
chest pressed against my thighs,
staring at the tiles.
I take out the bottle of Lexomyl
and swallow a few little teeth
and shut my eyes.

I imagine them making their way
down my throat,
into my stomach,
and dissolving
into my bloodstream
and traveling to my brain.

Someone is outside, knocking,
waiting to get into the bathroom,
but I don't think I can move.
I don't think I can get off this seat
and go out there,
in the dark
with all those people
and all those courses.
Deep breaths.
Deep breaths.

175

I get off the seat
and put a wet paper towel on the back of my neck.
I am not sure how long I've been in here,
but I am hoping that somehow
I have missed the rest of the courses
and Rebecca and Robyn are ready to leave.

When I return to the table
it is set with the same course as when I left.
I am quiet and shaking,
waiting for the pills to hit.
When the shivering and shaking stops,
I know that I will be okay,
but my jaw is still tight
and my knees are knocking
and the only thing I can do is
stare at the candle flame
because it is constant.

Hearing new languages
and walking strange and unfamiliar streets
makes my head spin.
I should be happy and calm and vacationing
but instead I am taking sedatives.

176

It's hard to be in such close quarters
with someone who doesn't understand.
Robyn has never seen this side of me.
We met last semester
when things were good.
I'm afraid that Robyn thinks
I am being overly dramatic,
and that what is happening isn't a big deal.

"Claire, whatever that doctor gave me isn't cutting it.
I need something else.
I'm in Italy, and I don't know how
I'll find a doctor who speaks English.
No, I'm on a pay phone, you can't call me back.
Call your mom and ask her.
She's a therapist and knows about drugs.
I'll call you back in a little while.
I just need a name of a drug —
something she thinks would work,
so I can go in there and tell the doctor what I want,
what I need."

Xanax 1 mg
is like a roller coaster,
like whiplash.
I am okay for a little while
and then I snap back.

In Venice, I try to swallow it.
I try to push it down
to the pit of my stomach,
under my feet.
I have to pay attention.
Every moment
I must be on guard.

The coast of Italy blends back into France.
There is nothing but sky and water
and each is changing shades
of the same color.

This was supposed to be
one of the best times of my life
but it has been a nightmare
that only pills can stop.

178

I cannot explain how significant it is
to be tracing the outline of the coast.
I like this feeling
of being on the edge of something so big.

There is so much that I am supposed to be saying,
so much that I am supposed to be doing,
but instead I am sitting here picking
at my wounds, bringing up blood,
and looking behind my nails
to see what I have scraped up.

From the coast, everything gets put into perspective.
Going past thousands of homes I get smaller.
Looking at a sea that never seems to end
makes me disappear too,
but in the middle of all this
there is a small island
with a wooded mountain
with a house at the top.

Looking at myself
in a fragmented mirror in the bathroom
of the Hole in the Wall bar in Vieux Nice.
An eye here,
lips there,
all misplaced and disjointed,
all make sense.

Two days with Xanax.
Two days without attacks.
Maybe this is the best way —
twice a day,
little white pills for calm and quiet,
for sense of a composed face
in a broken mirror.

V.

We are on the overnight train to Barcelona
and I am nervous
that Rebecca and I don't speak Spanish
and we aren't sure where to get off the train.
Early in the morning, before dawn,
we switch trains at Port Bou.
I see a group of young American guys
and figure one of them knows where to go.
We talk to them for the rest of the ride
and when we get off
they insist that we all stay at the same hostel.

When we get there
there is only one room left
with beds for five people.
We are stuck with them
because I wasn't confident
that we could manage on our own.

Rebecca and I spend the day
at Park Güell, designed by Gaudí.
All the structures rise up from the earth

181

like someone watered them and they grew.
I know this is the most beautiful place I have ever been,
but I cannot enjoy it.

That night the guys and Rebecca and I
are supposed to be going clubbing near Las Ramblas,
but as it gets later and we start to get ready,
I can't decide
if it would be worse to stay behind
with no one to talk to,
or to go, fearing I will have a panic attack.
But mostly all I can think about is Rebecca
and how I am ruining her spring break.

Even though I don't want to be alone,
it would be worse
to make Rebecca stay with me.
I insist that she go with them and have fun.
I have a book,
a CD player,
and a new box of Xanax
that I talked a pharmacist into giving me.

It is hard being alone,
sitting on the balcony

and watching the people below
being normal
and having fun.

I try to take a hot shower, to relax,
but the bathroom is filthy
and the water won't stay hot long enough
to enjoy it.
I must remember
all bad nights come to an end.
The pain eventually goes away.
I have cried more in the last two days
than I have in the last year.
The attacks keep coming,
and it hurts worse than anything else
that I can't stop them.

I take a Xanax,
get into bed,
hair still wet,
and cry until I fall asleep.

It's dark when I wake up
and they are back.
The guys are joking around,

183

being drunk,
trying to get me to get up,
but it's the middle of the night
and I was finally somewhere
that wasn't terrible.

One of the guys starts jumping on my bed
and another opens a can of beer
and it sprays all over me.
I feel like I am with a bunch of children.
All I want to do is sleep
and be left alone
and the only thing I can do
is scream and curse at them.

I realize that it has to be done.
I have to leave Barcelona,
go back farther than Paris or New York.
I tried to tell myself that it was going to be okay,
but it is not.
Even with the pills,
the terror still comes.

I don't think I look like myself anymore.
I feel like I tried to ignore too much
and now I am here shaking
in some strange city.

I don't feel connected to my body.
I feel racing and suspension all at once.
My breath is never even.
I have cold hands and knots in my stomach
that barely let up after another pill.
I have to face the fact that *it* is still there
and that may mean explaining to my parents
why I am home from France early,
and going back to therapy,
and getting new pills
because I am back to the point
where I will try anything.

It is finally time to accept
that I am not as solid
as I would like to believe.
I cannot go on like this.
Each new attack damages me so much
that I am searching

for that perfect black hole
where I can hide out until it stops
and I can emerge into the sunshine
with only rubble at my feet.

So afraid to go outside,
to be happy,
to be with other people
because they do not understand what it is like.

I am fearful of romantic dinners,
huge crowds, dusk —
of normal things —
afraid to be loved,
the one thing I want most.
Maybe it's because I don't think that I deserve it
because I am not that perfect
little girl that I was supposed to be,
well manicured and well groomed,
because I have nervous breakdowns,
and take pills,
and keep moving.

I am tired
and two years overdue
for a nap that can fix this.

The decision has been made.
Rebecca and I will go back to Paris
for a few days to gain peace and quiet,
to see if I can continue traveling
without losing my mind.

This is one of the hardest decisions
I have ever had to make —
next to the first time I went on medication —
because it's admitting
that I am sick.

I am up early,
letting Rebecca sleep in
before we leave —
a consolation prize.
I go for a walk
even though I am scared I'll get lost.

187

I need air.
I need to move.

I cross the square
and walk down the street.
Each step I take is small, cautious,
but it feels good
to be able to do this,
to be brave
and be alone.

I go into a perfume shop
and breathe it all in.
It feels good
to be overwhelmed by scents
and not fear.
The smells are comforting.
Heavy ones make me think of my mother.
Spicy ones, my sister.
Sharp musk, my father.
Some are like clean laundry,
others like lemons.
I find one that smells like honeysuckle —
like my parents' backyard —

and buy it.
I deserve a present.

It's a sick joke,
making this decision,
disappointing myself,
disappointing Rebecca,
accepting defeat
and finding all the trains to Paris booked.

This is a nightmare.
Spain is a cage.
I told myself that getting out would help,
and now I can't.
We are back at the hostel
and my tail is between my legs

On the phone in Paris with my parents
I cover the receiver as I cry.
"We're back because we pushed ourselves too much —
tried to do and see too much too quickly."
This is too hard.
"We are exhausted."

189

I am exhausted.
"We are going to hang out in Paris for a few days
before we go to Biarritz."
I am going to try and pull myself together.
"Yeah, everything's great.
Love you. See you in a few weeks."
I don't think I can do this.

I don't want to leave Paris.
The thought of traveling makes me sick
and even after two Maalox
my stomach still isn't calm.
As Rebecca and I search through the travel guide
to find somewhere to stay,
I know that I don't have the strength to leave Paris,
to pack a bag and board an uncomfortable train.
But I am going.
I know if I don't leave Paris this weekend,
if I can't find it in myself to try,
I will die.

From the Biarritz train station,
we take a bus
to the middle of nowhere —
not even a place to get a bottle of water.
We wait
for the next bus
that will take us to the coast.

On the next bus,
we ride through dried up, flat land
and I think, I don't know how
I'm going to survive
the next few days.

It's absurd
that this is a struggle.
We are staying just a few minutes
from a gorgeous beach
in a hostel that looks like a tree house.
This is a dream.

Students dream about this.
I dreamed about this.
I am lucky enough to have this chance,

to have parents who will pay for me to be here,
and it is all wasted.

I don't want to let on to Rebecca
that things aren't good,
so I try to stay quiet,
and take my pills
like a good little girl.

We spend the rest of the day on the beach
and the night at the hostel bar.
There are people here
from all over the world.
There is one guy
who keeps looking at me
and when I go over toward him
he motions for me to sit down.
He is French and deaf.
I know the sign language alphabet
so we sign our names to each other.
We sit together for the rest of the night.
He reads lips,
and we draw pictures
and make gestures to communicate.

It takes so much energy and concentration to be with him
and understand what he is trying to say
that I forget
what is wrong with me.

vi.

After a week in Paris
I go back to normal.
I ride the metro to class,
wander the city,
feel trapped in my body,
eat dinner with my family,
spend all my money on clothes.

My parents are here.
They are staying at a fancy hotel
across from the Louvre.
I take the elevator up to their room
and follow the flowers on the carpet
to their door.
I feel like I am going to explode.
I am so happy to see them,
but I am scared
it will make me crack.
Everything I have been holding in —
everything they don't want to know —
will come gushing out
and never stop.

My father opens the door.
For the first time in my life
he has grown a beard
and I'm surprised
at how gray it is.
He looks so different
that it's hard to focus on him.
My mother is on the bed.
The first thing she says is,
"Why did you do that to your hair?"
The gates break
and I am crying.
Why would she say that first?
How will saying that
do anything but hurt my feelings?
My father tells me it looks cute
and runs his hand over the back of my head
where it's really short.

We spend the week together.
During the day we go to museums.
We go shopping.
We go out to dinner.
My mother speaks a little French,

but I am our navigator.
I can feel their pride
as I order our food
and talk to salespeople in French.
Robyn is also in town
and she's staying at my apartment.
I spend my nights with her
going to bars and clubs.
I am constantly exhausted
and on the edge of panic.

At the end of the week
my parents and I are in a restaurant
and my stomach is a mess.
I stare down at my full plate
and think, I have never been this tired.
I cannot even chew.
My body is empty
and no matter what I give it,
it is not enough.

I tell my parents I am sick.
I need to leave.
When the proprietor clears my untouched plate
she is confused and offended.

She wants to know
why I didn't eat anything
and it takes all my energy to reassure her
that I'm not leaving because of her food.

My last week in Paris
I get mail.
The envelope is small
and the handwriting is perfect,
yet masculine.
I turn it over.
There is no return address —
only a New York post office stamp
and my parents' zip code on the front.
It is from Jason
or Nate.
I hold it in my hands,
weigh it,
trying to figure out who it is from —
who I want it to be from.

I sit down
and open it.
Folded up into a neat square

are three notebook pages
filled, front and back.
I take in the handwriting.
It is Jason's.
My heart sinks.
I wanted it to be from Nate.
But when I flip it over to see the signature
I see I am wrong.
I read the letter
over and over
and over
and don't even tell Rebecca
what was written in it.
It is mine.

I'm leaving France before everyone else.
Most people are going to travel
or at least spend their last days in Paris partying.
As soon as classes are over
I am getting on a plane.
I can't stay here anymore.
I need to go home.
I need to go to sleep.
I need to sit still.

Ann found an apartment for us
for the summer by school.
Each day I am going to ride my bike
for a half mile, past all the mansions
and lawn jockeys, to work at school
in the Events Department.
Everything about this summer
is going to be quiet
and slow.

vii.

I am at my parents' for a week
before I move to school.
It is strange to be back in the States
and to have everything change so quickly.
Life was so frenetic in Paris
and as soon as I walked in my parents' door
everything came to a full stop.
Back in my own country,
with my own language,
I still feel alone,
like no one understands me.

I spent so much time in Paris
wishing I were home,
in a safe place,
but now that I am here,
it is as hard as being away.
I don't know what to do with myself.
It is hard to sit down and do nothing.
I watch TV, do errands,
but this pace makes me feel
like my heart is going to stop.

I sit in my room
and reread my journals from high school
and cry because my biggest problem then was Jason.
How did I get so far from that
and so close to this feeling in my belly —
the feeling that this skin isn't good enough,
that it doesn't quite fit,
that anyplace is better than here?

My parents see how battered I am.
It is hard to miss.
I tell them that the change of pace is too hard on me.
That coming back was a shock to my system.
My mother takes me to a family doctor
to get a new prescription
and tries to convince me
not to move to school for the summer.
But I have to go.
I can't stay here.

Klonopin 0.5 mg.
This orange bottle
and these yellow pills

are so familiar.
In return for the prescription
the doctor makes me promise
that I will see a therapist
at school.

Thinking about Provence scares me.
To me, walking up and down that path,
bending over, grasping my head, crying
because I couldn't make it stop
is the face of insanity —
uncontrollable panic and fear,
the nonstop rush and no way out.
All I could think about
was how I didn't deserve this,
and that I was a good person,
and how much it hurt.

I feel like a different person
compared to that girl.
I can barely recall the way it felt —
a blessing, I suppose.
Why would I want to remember it vividly?

I have only a general sense of the pain,
of not being able to control my body
and my thoughts.
All I ever wanted
was to have control —
to be in charge of myself
and the rest of the world.

When I look back at my pictures from Europe
will I forget how much everything hurt?
Will it all not seem so bad?
Will the attacks be shorter?
Will there be fewer?
Will I have them at all?
When I see a picture of me
standing in front of a canal in Venice
or waving at the camera in the markets of Florence
and my color is a little off
and I have only a half a smile
will I think it is because the lighting was bad
or the camera caught me
just before I could smile?
I have to be careful what I remember.
It wasn't all good.

Things are already so different.
My memory cannot be trusted.

I want to be with Nate so badly.
I want to sit down with him
and have him put his arm around me
and tell me that he loves me,
even if he doesn't.
But I can't even get him
on the phone long enough
to tell him what's happening to me
and how awful Paris was
and how awful it is to be home,
to be anywhere.

I sit in the TV room and stare at the phone,
wondering how long it will take
for him to call me back,
wondering how long
before I can call him again.

Like always I cave and call.
I tell him I need him.
I tell him I need him now.

204

He tells me that he is waiting
for one of his friends to come over —
one of his stupid wasted friends.
I need him.
Why is not disappointing his loser friend
more important than seeing me,
helping me?
He says, "Samantha,
I know you are very angry with me,
but I can't do anything about it right now."
There is something about how slowly
and calmly he says it,
how he enunciates every syllable,
that makes me slam the phone down
over and over again.

Now I'm back staring at the phone
thinking how I've never hung up on anyone
and how I never even got the chance
to tell him what was wrong.

My first apartment
has thick brown shag carpeting
that traps the heat and smells of cat.

Like other apartments,
we have pots and pans,
but these are my pots and pans.
That is my blender.
This is my room.

We have a balcony
facing the town's main street.
Ann and I sit up there
and watch the sun set.
I blow bubbles
just to watch the people below
laugh and look around, confused.

Lately I've been thinking a lot about eating,
or how I'm not eating enough.
I don't think I'm getting enough nutrition.
I bought some dietary supplement shakes,
not the kind to make you lose weight,
but the kind old people drink to stay healthy.

Things are calm.
I set my own pace here.
I swim at the lake with friends,
meet Ann and her boyfriend

for happy hour after work,
go to barbecues that last for hours.
This is my routine.
The only thing I don't like
is my bike ride home from work.
It's all downhill
and the speed scares me.

I have an appointment
with a therapist.
I spend the day before the appointment
thinking about the things I am afraid of:
That I will be alone.
That no one will love me.

But are these really the fears I worry about?
What about not succeeding?
Not pleasing my parents?
Being left alone, with no one to help me,
just in case something terrible happens?

The new fear
of not being able to get out
has affected me worse than all the others.

It is much more crippling.
I cannot shake Provence, no matter how hard I try.
But do I really try hard enough
to take down my walls?
I wonder if I am too close
to even see what is written on them.
This close, everything is just a blurry mess.

The session with the new therapist is exhausting.
We start from scratch.
I tell him about myself,
about my sister and my parents,
the names of all the drugs I've taken,
how my anxiety is worse at night,
and that Europe was a disaster.

We talk about how I fear
losing control,
how I fear embarrassment,
how I fear fear.

I try to be optimistic,
but I can't believe that I am back here,

in this chair,
telling all my stories, hoping
that this time
will be the last time
I have to do this.

Part IV

Part IV

i.

Rebecca, Ann, and Jennifer
and I are living in an off-campus apartment
that's a converted bed-and-breakfast.
We each pay five hundred dollars a month
and have our own bedroom and bathroom.
I know this is not reality.
My parents pay my rent
and my credit card bills for food.
My only responsibilities are
to write poetry, take pictures,
write papers, and take my medication.
My life is so easy now
and I wonder what it will be like
in the spring when I graduate.

What kind of job do I want?
Where am I going to live?
My parents have spent
so much money on my education
and I don't have any idea
what I am going to do when I leave here.

I have the dream again.
My sister and I are crossing the Pont Neuf,
a bridge in Paris,
when I realize my mouth is filled
with tiny black rocks.
I sit down and start spitting them out.
I tell my sister not to worry —
that this happens all the time.

My therapist and I work
on relaxation.
He tells me to close my eyes
and imagine I am in a comfortable, safe place.
He wants me to focus on my breathing,
but I can't do it.
I'm not ready
to shut my eyes again.

We talk and I ask
if he knows any books that would help me.
I am eager to do something tangible
to help my anxiety.
He orders me an anxiety workbook.
It will be filled with exercises

214

and ways to take control of my anxiety.
When it comes I never use it.

The therapist sends me to a psychiatrist
to manage my meds.
This psychiatrist is not like the others.
He wears faded jeans
and black Converse sneakers
that he puts up on his desk.
He thinks Paxil will be better than Klonopin
and I am in no position to disagree.

Paxil 10 mg
makes me want to vomit
every hour of every day.
When I brush my teeth,
it makes me gag.
When I put a pencil between my teeth,
it makes me gag.
The psychiatrist tells me to tough it out,
that the side effects will pass.
I give it two weeks.

215

Serzone 200 mg
is not bad.
The hardest part is remembering
to take it in the morning
since I've always taken my meds at night.

None of my friends can understand
how the last three years went so quickly.
It feels like the first day of freshman year
wasn't that long ago —
like we just met and are still trying
to find our way around campus.
But now we are seniors.
We are at the top of the heap.
Everyone is looking up toward us,
but I am looking back.

I wonder how I could have done things differently —
how I could have done things better.
Did I take the right classes
and have the right major?
Did I choose English because it was easy for me
or could I have pushed myself more
and done something else?

216

I think about how I never went out enough
and how I should have been more social
and gone to more parties.
I think about girls who found love here,
if only for a little while,
and I feel like I missed out.

Ann and I are home,
alone in the apartment
after a Halloween party,
and I am high.
I haven't smoked pot in months,
but I took a few cautious hits at the party
since my anxiety has been better.

Ann and I watch a DVD
and eat doughnuts until we are stuffed.
We say good night and go to our rooms
to get ready for bed.

In the shower the water sounds like an avalanche.
That's when I realize I am too high
and that there is nothing
I can do about it but wait.

217

My mind is racing
and I can't stop thinking
about how I am too high,
and that it's going to make me crazy,
that it is going to make my heart stop,
and that the water is too hot,
and the sound of the water is deafening.
I try to wash my hair,
but I keep dropping everything.
First the shampoo,
then the conditioner,
then the bar of soap.
I can't hold on to anything.
Ann's shower is on the other side of the wall.
She bangs hard on the wall,
yells to see if I am okay.
I say yes,
but I'm not.

My therapist wants to know
how my panic attacks serve me.
I don't understand.
He wants to know what I gain from them.
Gain?

He thinks they serve a purpose.
I still don't understand.
Is he saying that I do this to myself
to avoid situations I don't want to be in?
To myself?
I am crying as I talk
and there must be little threads of spit
connecting my upper and lower jaw.
To myself?
I have never heard anything so awful in my life.

Thanksgiving with my parents
is surprisingly easy.
My parents decided not to make a fuss this year
and take us to Montreal.
We are going to stay in a fancy hotel
and have dinner at a four-star restaurant.
We stay in adjoining rooms
and spend the day walking around the city,
going to galleries, and shopping.
Everyone is happy.

Thanksgiving dinner is sterile.
The atmosphere is nice,

the food is good,
but something is missing.
There shouldn't only be four of us.
I would rather be at my parents' house
listening to my father yelling at my mother
to sit down with her guests,
and my mother yelling at my father
to get out of the kitchen,
and my mother's friend trying to make it seem
like her kids' accomplishments
are better than mine and my sister's.

I get back from the bars with my roommates
and get into bed.
I have the spins.
I only had two drinks —
it doesn't make sense
that I feel like I am on a rocking boat.
I sit up and the spins go away,
but as soon as I lie down again
they come back.
This feeling, the fact that I cannot make it stop,
is making me crazy.

It feels like I am having a panic attack,
like I am not in control of my body.

I go into the bathroom
and sit down in front of the toilet.
I've never had to make myself do this.
I almost never let myself drink to this point.
But tonight doesn't make sense.
I wasn't even drunk.
Maybe something else is wrong with me?
Maybe I have food poisoning,
or a virus,
or something that doesn't have a name.

I stare at the tiles.
I stare at the bowl.
I stare at the hair on the floor
that I should have cleaned up.
I stick my finger down my throat,
but it is not enough.
I only gag.
I try again,
stick my finger down farther,
be more brave.

This time everything comes up
and I can't make it stop.
The spins may be gone,
but now I can't control
the spasms in my stomach
that keep me retching.

When I am done,
I wash my face, brush my teeth,
and go into Rebecca's room.
I am twenty years old,
I should be able to handle this on my own,
but I can't.
I don't want to.

For work-study
I've been helping out an English teacher
with copying and research.
Now he's planning a presentation
for teachers from nearby towns
and needs me to act out a scene from a book
by crouching on a table like a monkey.
It'll be in the largest lecture hall on campus —
one that I've had panic attacks in

because it was always crowded and quiet
and I was scared that people were looking at me,
knowing I was freaking out.
I can't believe I agreed to do this
and put myself in a position
where people will definitely be staring at me
while I do something ridiculous.

I psych myself up for it all week.
I tell myself that it will be a good experience —
that it will help me get over some of my fears
and that maybe
it's a step to reclaiming spaces
that were once scary to me.

When I am finally standing in the lecture hall
and we are about to start,
my hands are shaking.
I am going to look like such an ass.

But I tell myself, it's okay.
I am supposed to look like an ass.
People are going to laugh because it's funny.
No one is going to think that I am crazy,
but all these people's eyes on me is uncomfortable.

I don't like being the focus,
but I do it.
Both hands on the table, then a foot,
then the other foot,
and then I am crouching.

That's it.
It lasts a few seconds
and is over.
It's not a big deal.
People laugh because it's funny,
not because something is wrong with me.
When it's over,
I am energized.
I could do it again.
Fuck this room —
it's just a bunch of seats
filled with people I don't know,
people whose opinions of me don't matter,
people I will never see again.

Winter break is death.
It's all I can see.
A friend of the family has killed himself.

224

I am sitting next to my mother
when we get the call —
the kind of call you know isn't going to be good
before you even pick it up.

I loved Howie.
When I talked about him
I called him my cousin,
but he was more like an uncle.
He's known me since I was a kid
and has been there for everything —
my bat mitzvah, my high school graduation,
all the holidays, all the dinners.

The morning of the funeral
two of my parents' friends are at our house.
We are all going to the funeral together.
Everyone has their idea
about why Howie jumped out of his office window.
My mother just read an article
about how antidepressants have been linked to suicide
and she thinks that must be what happened.
My mother's friend, a lawyer, thinks that his death
must be related to Howie's law practice —
that Howie got into some sort of trouble

that he couldn't get out of.
When I try to tell him
that it is not for us to know,
that is not for us to try to understand
what Howie must have felt,
he brushes me off, tells me I am immature,
that people do things for a reason.

Upstairs, my sister comforts me.
She says she hopes that when Howie was falling
he felt like he could fly.

At the funeral
his wife of three months
makes noises that aren't human.
At the graveside
his mother steps forward,
fills the shovel,
and slowly sifts the dirt over the casket
as his father watches.

ii.

Going to the spring formal
marks another ending,
another thing that my friends and I
will never do again.
I watch everyone move around the banquet hall.
They go from the bar to the buffet
to the bar to the dance floor
and back to the bar.
Everyone is drunk and falling over themselves.

My stomach starts, just like that.
First there are sharp pains in my side
that come and go.
Then I get sweating hot
and goose-bump cold.
I take deep breaths and try to let it pass,
but the pain deepens.
I am going to be sick.
In the bathroom
there are girls in fancy dresses
wiping their mouths after puking
and fixing their makeup.

I pull up my skirt and sit on the toilet,
press my chest against my thighs,
and stare at the tiles
and wait to be sick.
I wait,
but nothing happens.

The pain subsides and I get some water
and go back to the patio where my friends are.
They ask how I am, but it's old news.
They've all seen this happen before.
When the pain comes back
I ask my friends not to leave the patio.
I tell them I'll be back in a few minutes.

In the bathroom
I take my seat,
put my chest on my thighs,
my chin on my knees,
wrap my arms around my calves,
and get sick.

When I get back to the patio
they are all gone.
I look by the bar.

No one.
I look by the buffet.
No one.
I was only gone a few minutes.
Why wouldn't they wait?
I look on the dance floor.
No one.
I know they are still here,
but this place is too big.
I am never going to find them.
I go back to where they were last.
No one.
I asked them to stay
because I didn't want to end up alone,
searching for them.
I can't believe they would do this.
They knew I was sick.
They couldn't wait five minutes for me?
It's loud and crowded
and I am sick
and I want to leave
and I can't believe them.
When I run into some kids driving back to campus
I ask to go with them.

This is my out
and I am not going to let it pass.

As I am heading for the door
I see Rebecca.
I tell her I'm leaving.
She's confused about the urgency
and why I am so mad.
I ask her why they left the patio.
She apologizes,
says she didn't realize everyone was getting up.
But it doesn't matter.
I am taking my out.

My whole life has changed,
or at least I think it has.
It's hard to tell what would have been —
what I would have been,
if I never had anxiety disorder.

I never stay out very late.
My friends all understand —
they are with me enough
to see the complete picture,

230

but when I am out with acquaintances
they sometimes catch on
and see that I am always the first to leave.
It's like a timer goes off in my head
and I know it's time to go.
Maybe I am trying to outrun the panic.
I figure if I've made it
this long without panicking
then I shouldn't push my luck.

There are other things that I do.
I always have to be in control.
If I am going out with friends
I like to be the one who chooses where we go.
I have to know what we are doing,
where we are going,
how we are getting there,
and how long we'll be staying.

I don't remember being like this
in high school, before I was diagnosed,
and I hate that I don't know
if all these things are me
becoming me
or me because of the anxiety.

231

There's a banner in the student center
that counts down the days until graduation.
Today the banner says thirty-two.
I can't believe this is it.
This was college.
It's over.
I am leaving soon.

I try to send out my résumé,
but it's too soon.
They all tell me to call back
when I get home and can interview.
But waiting is killing me.
Don't they understand?
Don't they remember what it feels like?
I want to have things settled.
I can't stand the idea of not knowing.

I can't believe that I am doing this again.
Graduation is in a week
and I have to start packing.
I have moved more than ten times
in the last four years —

232

I just want to sit still.
I just want to be left alone.

Senior Week is about to begin.
I'm not looking forward
to a week of organized drinking.
If I could have my way
I'd stay home with my friends
and watch movies and bake cookies.

The night before graduation
my family and my parents' friends
go to dinner at a tiny restaurant.
I am exhausted
and this place is too dark and too loud.
How do people expect you to eat in the dark?
I am fading.
My stomach is in knots
and eating is out of the question.
I do not have the strength for this.
I am like a newborn
who cannot even hold up her head.
My father jokes,

puts his elbow on the table
and palm out for me to rest my head on.
I lean against his warm hand,
breathe in his cologne,
and shut my eyes.

Graduation morning is cold.
The ceremony takes too long
and all my friends and I
are freezing in our summer dresses.
There are too many speakers,
too many names called,
and in the end,
we don't even get our diplomas —
that comes later, in the mail.

There is hugging
and pictures,
and introducing my parents to
friends and teachers.
And that's it.
It is over.
All that's left to do
is put my stuff in the car.

Part V

i.

All those garbage bags
and plastic bins are back in my room
and instead of being yelled at to pack,
I am being yelled at to unpack.
It doesn't seem right to be here —
in this house,
in this room
with this stupid flowered wallpaper,
but I have no where else to go.
I have no money.
I have no job.

My parents allow me
one week before I have to start job hunting.
I want more time.
I want to relax
and be with my friends,
but when the week is up,
my dad leaves the classifieds in my room.

I look for a job,
but I don't know what I want to do.

I don't know what I can do.
I make phone calls and send out my résumé
for jobs that I'm not sure I want.
No one calls me back.

After two unsuccessful weeks
I take a temp job at a hedge fund.
I'm not interested in finance,
but it pays well.
I make phone calls and copies.
I go to the drugstore
to get my boss's prescriptions
and look up what they're for on the Internet.
Weeks pass and all I learn
is to stay out of my boss's way
when the stock market does badly.

After a few weeks
I get a job at a publishing house.
The pay is terrible, but at least it's a career —
something I can see myself doing
for more than a few weeks.
The work is still crap.
I still make phone calls and copies,

but at least now
the product is something tangible,
something I can be proud of.
I can deal with all the busywork,
but my boss is awful.
She rubs all my mistakes in my face
like a dog that shit on the rug.
She treats me like an idiot,
like I don't have the right to a learning curve.
Most days I go home crying
and my dad tells me
welcome to the real world.

Fall is coming
and I feel like I've fallen off the map.
It's the first time in eighteen years
that I am not getting ready to go to school.
Since the age of three I've been on a track —
preschool, elementary school,
middle school, high school, college —
with never more than a summer in between.
I wish I could have waited
between high school and college.

I wish I could have moved more slowly,
but that wasn't part of the plan.

I have found myself talking about the weather a lot.
I think that means I have entered the real world,
that I am an adult,
because now I have awful gaps in time
to fill as I wait for trains and elevators
to take me to places I do not want to go.

This city is ugly
and the concrete is hard on my feet.
Everyone pushes and is angry
at the people who push them.

I am not happy.
I am not unhappy.
I am frozen somewhere in the middle
that is so much worse.
I am NOWHERE.
Nothing is happening
and I am getting more and more sad.

Is this what all the years of schooling were for?
To prepare me for this
sense of being stuck in the middle?
What was the point?
No one said I was going to be this sad.
No one said I would still be crying.

I am so lonely.
Every day is the same —
trying to move slower than the rest,
to not be so angry,
so serious in the morning,
to not make myself crazy.

I stand on the packed subway
jammed in, pushed too far
to hold on to the sticky poles.
There are bags pressing against my thighs,
hands touching mine,
a man's chest against my shoulder.
I would stay on the subway longer,
let the crowd rub up against me
as the subway rocks,
but I have to get to work.

241

I don't think that I am happy,
but then again, I don't know.
Sometimes I get so caught up
in the process of living —
of eating, dressing, taking the train to work,
that I don't give it enough thought.
Maybe happiness is being content.
But is this really it?

I am only twenty-one.
I have been out of college only a few months.
I don't want to have a job
that I think is merely all right.
But then I see street sweepers,
men polishing marble floors,
people selling magazines and nuts on the street,
and I think I am a spoiled brat.

I must have only been in remission
these last few months
because now the anxiety is back.
It made me stay home from work
and spend the day tiptoeing around myself —
not eating too much, or too little,

and drinking liquids, tons of liquids,
until I am hydrated, bloated.

Maybe this is happening
because I have grown tolerant
of my medication.
Maybe too many new things are happening.
Maybe this is just me,
and this is how my whole life will be.

I am scared
that I do not really want to get well,
and that I am the greatest obstacle to my recovery.
Why would I do this to myself?
Why would I inflict this much pain,
turn my life upside down,
twist my stomach in knots,
run from friends, family,
even from entire countries?

Shit, I feel sick.
All this makes me sick.
I am a good person.
I know I am beautiful

243

and that I love
and that I care.
It's the world, right?
The world has the problem, not me.
From Spain to the world —
I will not take blame for any of this.

I am in a house with three other people
and none of them can see me —
see what I am going through.
It's late and I am in bed.
I should be sleeping,
but it feels like my body is on fire.
The longer I stay by myself
the hotter I burn.
I go to my sister's room,
but she's not there.
I go past my parents' room
and quietly down the stairs.
My sister is always up late watching TV.
I know if I tell her
it will make the burn less hot.

I stand there and just look at her.
The corners of my mouth turn down
and I am crying,
shaking my head,
telling her that I am freaking out,
that I can't sleep.

She makes room for me on the couch.
Her arm is around me and she is touching my hair.
Telling her makes it better.
Knowing that I don't have to go through it alone
makes it less painful.

We watch TV for a long time
and she scratches my head
and I cry until I am tired
and can go upstairs
to sleep.

Sometimes
when I am walking down the street
I feel like a giraffe,
with my knees pointed backwards.

As soon as the train doors close
I know this is a mistake.
My heart is racing.
I can't breathe.
And this might be it.
This might be the time
that I cross the line
from outpatient to inpatient.
I can't sit still.
I can't be on this train.
I look out the window
and take long, slow breaths.
I wish I had water.
I wish I had something to read.
Long
slow
breaths.
I shouldn't be on this train.
I should be at home.
I want to get off at the next stop
and have my sister come and get me.
No.
Deep breaths.
I promised Rebecca
I would go to a party with her.

No.
I can't do this.
I can't go to a party
and pretend to be normal.
I am bouncing my foot
up and down
because at least that is something.
We are almost to the city,
but it is taking too long.
I am going the wrong way.
I should be going home.
I call my sister,
tell her I am having a panic attack,
tell her I don't know what to do.
She tells me to calm down.
She tells me she'll come and get me from the city,
but I want there to be someone with me
here, now.
I don't want to wait.
I can't wait
for her in Penn Station,
with all those people going past me
on their way to parties, and plays, and bars.
And what if she drives so fast
that she gets into an accident?

No.
I'll take the train back.
I call Rebecca,
tell her I'm sorry,
but I can't do it —
I have to go home.

I don't even need to change trains.
This train is going back where it came from.
But I have to wait —
wait for everyone to get off
and a new set of people to board,
wait for the conductor to announce the stops.
It is taking forever.
I am rocking back and forth a little
as if I were listening to music,
hoping that my movements
will propel this train into action.
Finally, the bell rings
and the doors shut.
For a second I feel trapped,
but I try to keep quiet inside
and remember this is what I want.

The ride back is better
than the ride there
because I know I am going home.
I know that my sister will be there,
that my parents will be there,
and that I will be safe,
but I am not there yet.
I have twenty-five minutes to go.
I want to get home as quickly as possible,
but the feeling of the speeding train is scary.
It feels like we are going too fast,
like the train is going to fall off the tracks,
land on its side, and crush us all
and these few people in the car with me
will be the last faces I ever see
and I wonder if we get into an accident
and if I am dying
if I will have enough strength left
to call my parents and sister on my cell phone
and tell them I love them.

I sit with my mother on the couch and cry.
She puts her cool hand on top of mine
and pats me lightly.

249

She looks back at me, sad.
It feels good that she knows,
that my father knows.
They want to know how they can help.
They ask me what I need
and they hug me longer
and it makes the pain less intense.
But it is still there,
relentless.

We sit in the living room
with the lights dim and we talk
about taking me to a hospital.
They want to know if I want to go.
They want to know if I want to stay.
They want to know if I want to eat,
but I have no wants.
I just lie toppled over on the couch
with my feet still on the floor
and my cheek pressed
against the sticky leather cushion.
I cry and wonder
how I'm going to fall asleep
because sleeping means waking
and going through all this again.

ii.

I am in that familiar seat
with a stranger staring at me
expecting me to tell him all my stories.
This sucks.
I barely get through a sentence
without crying.
Like always, I start at the beginning.
As I give the speech, I think
I might as well make a recording
since I keep having to repeat myself.
I am twenty-one years old.
Blah blah.
I was diagnosed with anxiety disorder
when I was seventeen.
Blah blah.
I have been prescribed blah blah and blah
and now I am back at the beginning
at home
and freaking out.

Serzone 300 mg
is my prize
for going back into therapy.

Going to see the new therapist
is a pain in the ass.
I take the train home from work
then the bus or a taxi for a mile.
My father picks me up afterwards,
when my face is puffy from crying
and my clothes are sticky
from all the sweating.

I'm not sure I like this therapist.
He talks too much —
sometimes it's about his kids,
sometimes about his other patients.
I try to be objective,
but I never see his point.

He tells me he is going to teach me
how to breathe.
He says it is the key
to managing my anxiety.

252

He gets out from behind his desk
and sits next to me on the couch.
He puts his hand on my stomach
as he counts for me
and tells me to take deep breaths.
I don't like that he does this,
but I am not sure what to say.

I am in overload.
I know that.
I can rationalize and pick apart
all the things that are wrong —
all the things that are making me freak out,
but that doesn't make the feeling go away.
I feel like crap.
I have my period.
I am exhausted.
My great-aunt died.
I hate my job.
I feel stuck at home.
One at a time
these things aren't a problem,
but when they're piled on
it leads to disaster.

Three steps forward
and two steps back.
It looks like I am making progress,
but I feel the backward pull —
pulling me toward how things used to be.
Now the attacks are snowballing.
One panic attack leads to two, two leads to three
until I am back in the dark place
where I hate everything.

Work sucks.
When I get back from taking the day off
to go to my great-aunt's funeral,
my boss doesn't even ask me who died.
I don't want to be here.
I don't want to have to take the train home
with all those other depressing commuters.
I wish I were at home, in bed,
but instead I am here,
filing and making copies.

A new girl just started in my department.
She looks like a pixie
and moves around the office

with almost no sound.
I know it would be nice
if I offered to show her around
or go over office procedures,
but I don't have the strength
to do anything for anyone
but myself.

Thanksgiving sucks.
We are at another fancy hotel,
except this place is not serene.
There is a glass ceiling
that makes the screaming kids
sound even louder.

The food comes, but I am not interested.
To avoid scrutiny
I work my way around the plate clockwise.
First, turkey.
Fork up.
Take bite.
Fork down.
Take sip of water.
Now, potatoes.

255

Fork up.
Take bite.
Fork down.
Take sip of water.
Maybe if I move at regular intervals
no one will notice that I am dying.

The more I see this therapist,
the more I dislike him.
Last week I told him
a story about when I felt like a slut,
but he didn't understand.
I am still a virgin —
how could I feel like a slut?

Today we talk about
how I need to be more organized.
He suggests I get a planner just like his.
He takes it out, shows it to me,
and tells me all the places I can buy it.
He goes on about it for twenty minutes.
I keep trying to change the subject
but he is oblivious.

No one ever tells you
that it's okay to not like your therapist
and that you don't have to keep seeing him
just because someone recommended you
or because he takes your insurance.

After a week of trying to figure out
how to dump him,
I leave a message on his machine,
saying that things just aren't working out
and spend the day wondering
if he thinks I'm passive-aggressive.

I am filled with such sadness
and I am so tired
that I could die.
The only music
I can stand to hear
is Billie Holiday.

I cannot face my friends,
or anyone else,
and I sat for so long in the shower
that my hands are raw and cracked.

257

I do not feel like myself,
and if this is me,
then something needs to change.

I fear my whole life
will be exactly like this —
seen from behind my eyes,
never touching.

I am scared to sleep.
I am scared to eat.
I am scared to move.
And all this turns my stomach
and reminds me how alone I am
and how pitiful it is
that I need someone to love me,
to wrap me up and make me feel safe,
and how pathetic it is
that I can't find someone, anyone
to do that for me.

I am waiting
in the waiting room
of the new therapist's office.

There is a drawing on the wall
of a guy in a strange hat.
This is not an ordinary drawing.
This is a portrait.
I am supposed to know who this is.
I search his face.
Nothing.
When I look at his hat again
I realize it is in the shape of windmill.
This is Don Quixote —
a deluded literary character
who fights for the honor of a woman
who doesn't exist
and does battle with monsters
that are really windmills.
I'm going to like this therapist.

Each week I get more and more medicated.
On my first visit, the new therapist
raises my dose of Serzone 100 mg.
The next week, I am not any better
and I get another 100 mg.
One more week,
another 100 mg.

259

600 mg and I am maxed out
and things still suck, only now,
I am having problems with my balance.

Now I must taper off
the same way I went on.
Tuesday, 600 mg.
Wednesday, 500 mg.
Thursday, 400 mg.
Friday, 300 mg.
Saturday, 200 mg.
Sunday, 100 mg.

Celexa 10 mg
will be better than Serzone,
my new therapist says.
We start low
and I work my way up again.
The first week I take 10 mg.
The second week I take 20 mg.
The week after that 30 mg.
My therapist cuts me off at 40 mg.

Ativan 0.5 mg
is sitting in a bottle in my room,
is floating in my wallet,
is crumbling in the back pocket of my jeans.
My therapist prescribed it
for when the attacks become unbearable,
but I don't want to take it.
I'm scared I will become dependent
and end up worse off than I am now,
but I keep it with me
just in case.

I have the dream again,
this time with Saran Wrap.
I am standing in front of a deli counter
when I realize I have a piece of Saran Wrap in my mouth.
I begin to pull it out.
I feel it unraveling
from somewhere inside my stomach
and dragging up my throat
and out my mouth.
I'm terrified I'm pulling out my intestines.

261

My parents have taken control of my life.
When I am not at work
my parents lead me around
like a sick animal.
I never go out on the weekends
with friends anymore.
I stay home and watch TV,
but never the news —
it hurts too much.
I don't bother to call my friends back —
not even Claire.
There is nothing to say.

My mother says, "Get up,
we're going to a flute concert."
I don't want to go to a flute concert.
I don't want to leave the house.
I don't want to sit in a room full of people
in the dark
and have to be quiet.
But I do not have it in me to protest.
I get dressed
and we go
and I cry.

My mother says, "Get up,
put on a skirt,
we are going to temple."
I don't want to go to temple
and sit quietly and pray.
But I do not have it in me to protest.
At temple I sit next to my mother
with a prayer book closed in my lap
and I cry.

I feel like a mental patient
on leave from the home.
It's strange.
I spent most of the last few years
trying to get out of going places with my parents,
but now I don't mind our outings.
Now it is comforting.
Now it is safe.

The therapist says I should keep a log
of when I have panic attacks.
He wants me to write down
where I was, what I was thinking

just before and during the attack,
and how long it lasted.

I don't like this idea.
It is too much focus
on something I am trying to forget.
I am afraid
that this attention to detail
will only fuel my anxiety.

I hate that I want to open up
my mouth and empty the bottle of Celexa
down my throat
and feel soft and quiet.

I'm not talking about suicide.
I just wish I were how I was before —
how I was my senior year in high school
when I didn't care
who liked me and who didn't,
how I was finally free.
Now I feel more bound than ever —
bound by this disease,
bound to repeat the behaviors

and thoughts
that are killing me.

I am the crazy friend.
Rebecca calls to check up on me
and to see if she should visit.
I am the patient
and she wants to know the visiting hours.
That's how bad this is —
she'll even come to Queens.
I don't want to see anyone.
I just want to sit at home
and watch TV with my sister
and have my parents pour wine for me at dinner.

My therapist and I do breath work.
We stare at each other
from matching green leather chairs.
I shut my eyes and he counts slowly for me.
"Breathe in,
two,
three.
Breathe out,

265

two,
three."
I try to focus
on filling my chest up with air
and instead of sucking air in,
I let my stomach balloon out.
I imagine my diaphragm
moving up and down,
like how you shake out a sheet
before you fold it.
"In,
two,
three.
Out,
two,
three."
Relaxing,
feeling
only
my
breath.
Only
hearing
his
voice.

I wonder what my life would be like
if I'd never had anxiety disorder.
At first I think, shit,
I'd be Miss America.
I'd be the happiest person
with the brightest smile on the face of the earth.
But the more I think about it,
the more scary life without panic seems.
My life has been governed by anxiety
for the last five years.
It fills up my time.
The practice of doing nothing —
of staring at walls and letting my mind go —
is torture.
I don't know how to live like that.
I only know how to live like this —
with this feeling in my stomach.

But this is no way to live —
fearing everything,
being scared to be me,
to be happy,
to feel pain.

There are so few things left inside me
besides fear.
The thought of having to go back to work —
having to go back out there,
knowing that this is my life,
that I am not happy,
that I expect more,
that I want more,
makes me sick.

When I have a panic attack
the voice in my head says
anything can happen.
I will go insane,
I will die,
I will start screaming,
I will piss all over myself.
I try to tell myself that that voice isn't real,
but it's hard.
The voice is very convincing.

I need to find a voice that is stronger —
one that is so rational
that it will cancel the other one out.

What does it take to believe
that I am going to make it?
Whose voice is good enough?
Is my own?
I write a note to myself,
put it in my wallet
and hope.

Where you are
and what you are doing
is something you have done
dozens of times before
without having any problems.

Recognize that you are going to get out of this —
that you always get out of this,
that you are going to live,
that you won't go crazy.

I am telling you that you will live,
because you always live,
because you are strong
and beautiful.

The therapist and I play a new game.
When I say, "I thought I was going to have a panic attack,"
he says, "So what if you did?"
He is mentally prodding me
from across the room.
I say, "It would suck
and I would think I was going crazy
and I would feel like I couldn't breathe."
"And . . . ?" he asks.
I say, "I might pass out."
"And . . . ?"
I already see where this is going.
It's a trap.
He is letting me use my words
against myself.
I say, "I'd wake up."
I hate this game.

I dream that I have cancer.
I go to the gynecologist
and he tells me that I have a week to live.
I don't understand.
I feel fine.
I have no symptoms.

How could I be carrying around
that much rot and disease
in my uterus and not even know?
I'm too young, I think.
I haven't done anything yet.

Later in the dream
things get bad quickly.
My parents and sister
rush me to the hospital
because I'm pissing blood.
I'm going to have surgery,
but the doctors don't think
I have much of a chance.

I lie on a table, under anesthesia.
My body is cold, but my mind is awake.
My father is preparing me for surgery,
but it feels more like for burial.
I am ashamed to be naked in front of him,
but he carefully washes my body
and cleans under my nails
and I scream for him inside my head.

All I can think is, I told you so.
I told you that my panic was real.
I told you that things like this happen.

I have a theory,
I tell my therapist while we talk about
my irrational fears regarding illness
and other catastrophes.
I call it the Post-it theory.
For every fucked-up thing that happens
I make a mental note.
There is a Post-it in my brain
for when Joelle died of meningitis.
There is a Post-it for when
my mother's friend had a brain tumor.
There are Post-its
based on things I hear in the news
and stories friends tell me.

If I have a bad headache,
part of me says, take some aspirin,
have some tea, take a nap.
But there is another part of me,
the part with all those Post-its lined up,

that says, no,
this is not a headache,
this is something larger,
something strange,
something that will kill you.

I try to tell myself,
what are the chances?
I am a healthy girl.
But those Post-its remind me
that things can happen —
that they do happen.

It is so hard to know
this kind of fear —
this level of irrationality —
because it opens all doors.
It finds the spiders in the corners
of every room —
the ones that are there
and the ones that aren't.
But shouldn't a limitless possibility of bad
open the spectrum
for a limitless possibility of good?

There are five days
between me and my last attack.
I feel like I am in AA.
I am counting the days,
hoping to get enough space
to feel like a different person,
a normal person.
Being at work has helped
keep me busy, occupied
long enough to forget how bad it was
a week ago,
how bad it was
a year ago.

Even though I am out of the hole,
I can still feel it.
I am a little quieter,
a little more cautious,
a little less made up,
and I wonder when it will hit again.

Each day without fear is a triumph.
The more space I can put between
myself and the last attack,

274

the stronger I feel.
I am proud of the distance,
but it makes me sick to think about it —
how it is still there,
how it has been there for so long,
how I am affected.

I wonder when I will be free,
when there will be days without pain,
but all this is dependent on me working hard
and telling the truth
and not being scared anymore.

I have moved out of the incredibly sad place
that I've been in for months.
It still creeps up on me,
but for the most part
it is gone.
It would seem that losing the sadness
would be a good thing,
but it has been replaced by nothing —
a quiet acceptance of this boring,
everyday life.
I think it's even worse

than being miserable.
At least miserable is active.

Today is my twenty-second birthday
and things don't seem so bad.
I just dyed my hair red
and I am having a party
at a bar called Double Happiness.
I feel better
and I wonder if it's because of the new meds,
or because of the new therapist.
Or maybe this is just another remission.
But I don't really care why.
All I care about is that things are better.

I take the train into the city
and a touch of anxiety comes over me.
What if no one shows up?
What if I have a panic attack and want to leave?
I take a few deep breaths
and remind myself that tonight is going to be fun
and it calms me.

At the bar it is hard to believe
that all these people are my friends.
Person after person filters in
as I preside at a table in the back.
I've never felt like this before.
I am at the center of attention,
and not because I am having a panic attack
or passing out at a concert.
It's just me
and the people I care about most.
Rebecca, Claire, Robyn, and Rachel are here.
Audrey drove in from Rhode Island.
A bunch of other kids from school came
and some kids I grew up with.
That guy from my poetry class is here,
flirting, vying for my attention,
and it is wonderful.
The only people missing are my sister
who is away on business
and Nate and Jason,
but that's not new.

It's after three A.M. when the snow starts to fall.
By the time Audrey and I get to her car

the snow is coming down even harder.
As soon as Audrey turns the key in the ignition,
Edith Piaf blares from the stereo.
I laugh at Audrey as we pull away,
and laugh even harder
when the car starts thumping down Mott Street.
We have a flat tire.
It's late, but it doesn't matter.
I told my parents not to expect me before 4 A.M.
and for once they didn't seem to mind.

At a gas station, Audrey and I wait
and watch the snow fall
as an attendant puts on the spare.
I don't mind the cold —
it's all part of the adventure.

Audrey and I head home in the blizzard,
going thirty miles an hour on the Long Island Expressway,
laughing and listening to Edith Piaf a little too loud,
and it doesn't matter
that I don't understand a word she's saying.

I went to yoga today.
I moved slowly
and did things carefully
and made sure to breathe.
It feels good to do something
alone, that is just for me.

It's New Year's Day.
My resolutions are
to actively work at finding happiness,
to be healthier,
more flexible,
more relaxed in my own skin —
comfortable, soft.

I feel stronger.
I am farther from the panic,
but I am still stuck
in my old patterns.
I wait for the clock
to strike a new hour
so I can leave parties
and do not check my coat

just in case I need to make a quick escape.
I've built myself safety nets,
but they bind me in a web.

I am in a house.
I am in one room
and my anxiety is in another.
It's close.
I can feel it.
I can go to it.
But I won't.

Author's Note

Why I Wrote This Book

The idea to write this book evolved out of a conversation with my psychiatrist when I was about twenty-three years old, nearly two years after the point this book ends. He asked how I'd been doing and if I'd had any panic attacks lately. I thought about it carefully and then realized it had been weeks since I had felt any surges of anxiety and months since I'd actually had a panic attack. How was that even possible? Only a few years before, I was having several panic attacks a day.

Even though I wasn't currently having problems with anxiety, I was living like I did. It still took a good amount of convincing to get me to go to places where I used to have panic attacks. I'd still go home earlier than my friends on a Saturday night. I clung to a few emergency pills in my purse just in case the anxiety became too much to bear. Things were better — but I didn't feel better.

In order to make sense of my lack of anxiety, in order to really feel it, I was going to have to quantify it. I thought that if I could remind myself of how bad things were in college, I could see how different — and how good — my life was now.

When I got home from my psychiatrist's office, I took out my college journals and started reading. I only had to read a few pages to see how bad things had been. The difference between "then" and "now" was stark.

I dug further through my old journals and did a lot of reflection. I also talked to friends, family, and my doctors to build a complete picture of those times. Then I started writing, incorporating some things from the journals and so much more from memory and research.

It was difficult in the beginning. I was very agitated and having trouble sleeping. But those feelings subsided as I pushed through and got into a rhythm of writing. Often it didn't feel like I was writing about myself. Instead, it was about this character who was eerily familiar. There was something transformative about looking at myself from far above while at the same time doing inward reflection.

The journey to write this book began with the intention of healing myself, but as I filled page after page and wrote poem after poem, I knew this book could provide comfort to others. I knew I wasn't alone in these feelings.

Bursting

A magical thing happens when the topic of my memoir comes up in conversation, and I open up about my experiences: The other person opens up too. Suddenly that person is telling me private things about themselves, their spouse, friend, or child who has struggled with mental health issues. It's as if that pain was sitting just below the surface of their skin waiting to break through. All they needed was to witness another person opening for them to burst. And with that bursting comes relief. Openness leads to connection. It leads to feeling less alone. Dealing with the pain and pressure of a mental health issue is challenging enough. But layer on top of it shame or secrecy? The burden becomes even heavier.

"Your book made me feel less alone" is by far the most common phrase I've heard in the letters and comments I've received over the years about my book. People have said how uncanny my words and experiences are. And to that I say: I am not special. And neither are you. We are all connected in a fundamental way. Anxiety, depression, loneliness, fear, grief, shame, anger? They sit in our bones. Wanting to feel accepted, safe, loved, and needed? That's streaming in our blood.

Now

Nearly fifteen years after the initial publication of *I Don't Want to Be Crazy*, my life looks so different from the pages in this book. I can hardly remember the last time I had a full-blown panic attack. There are still occasional things that trigger my anxiety. But I know what they are and I am pretty good at seeing the anxiety creeping up and catching myself before things get too far. Catching myself is key. If I can calm myself down before it snowballs, I've got a good shot of the intense anxiety lasting only a few moments.

Some things haven't changed though. I still go through periods where I want to be in therapy, but there have been plenty of months and years at a time where I don't feel like I need it. I'm still on medication and that's okay. I feel good. Feeling good is the goal. And the one thing that is definitely the same? Many of the people mentioned in this book are still by my side, loving and supporting me. And some new ones as well.

It's Okay to Not Be Okay

Everyone struggles. Anxiety and other strong emotions are a normal part of life. But when those emotions prevent us from living our lives fully, they take on a whole new context. One in five teens and young adults live with a mental health condition. Help is out there. I know it can be scary and maybe even embarrassing to tell someone you are struggling, but remember: This is not your fault. Asking for help is a sign of strength. If you had terrible back pain or got the flu, you'd go to the doctor, right? This isn't different. And the sooner you ask for help, the sooner you can start feeling better.

Make a list of the adults in your life that you trust. You can include your parents/caregivers, family members, family friends, teachers, spiritual leaders, your school nurse, or guidance counselor. Tell them how you're feeling. If they don't point you in the direction of help — or don't believe you need help in the first place — go to the next person on your list. If you get to the end of your list and still haven't found help, there are many online resources like mentalhealth.gov and NAMI.org.

I was able to ask for and get help, but I know that for some people finding the energy to do that while in so much pain can seem unimaginable. So don't just be there when someone asks for help. Make the call. Check in on someone if you think they're having a hard time. And for the people in your life who appear to have it all together? Ask them how they are too. You never know what's below the surface.

If you or someone you know is thinking about hurting themselves, call 911 immediately or the National Suicide Prevention Lifeline at 1-800-273-TALK. For additional resources visit my website at samantha-schutz.com. You are not alone. Help is out there. You can feel better.